Engineering
Healing of
HEARTBURN

The Story of a Physician-Patient
and Healing the Disease

JUDY GAO

authorHOUSE®

AuthorHouse™
1663 Liberty Drive
Bloomington, IN 47403
www.authorhouse.com
Phone: 1 (800) 839-8640

Published by AuthorHouse   08/24/2016

ISBN: 978-1-5246-1302-0 (sc)
ISBN: 978-1-5246-1301-3 (e)

Library of Congress Control Number: 2016911144

Print information available on the last page.

Any people depicted in stock imagery provided by Thinkstock are models,
and such images are being used for illustrative purposes only.
Certain stock imagery © Thinkstock.

This book is printed on acid-free paper.

Because of the dynamic nature of the Internet, any web addresses or links contained in
this book may have changed since publication and may no longer be valid. The views
expressed in this work are solely those of the author and do not necessarily reflect the
views of the publisher, and the publisher hereby disclaims any responsibility for them.

Contents

Contents

Introduction

In August 2012, after two months of viral bronchitis, I found myself struggling with what I thought at the time was simple heartburn. I was also under lots of stress from my busy clinical practice. My symptoms were peculiar, with many details that seemed unexplainable by a physician—myself. I found it was difficult to make a precise diagnosis. Even if I made a preliminary diagnosis, I could not figure out what was the exact etiology (i.e., what was causing this). I also had many trial treatments that were good in some ways, bad in other ways. With an engineering analysis and measurement approach and solution, I finally had a way to resolve my symptoms. You will share in my new greater understanding of the factors that lead to, cause, and respond to GERD (gastroesophageal reflux disease).

The pathway I systematically traveled is almost impossible to duplicate with current healthcare methods. This is because the pathway toward solutions for the individual will need many details communicated with your physicians during office visits in many treatment trials. This process requires many explanations from doctor to patient. You've probably experienced an interaction with your own doctor at some point when he or she was unable to tell you immediately exactly what was wrong with you. Sometimes your doctor can only guess or can give you a partial explanation. This is because there can be several possible causes for one specific symptom.

It is frustrating to leave an appointment with only a partial diagnosis and more questions than answers about why you are experiencing these symptoms. Doctors have their own language, and sometimes they forget to speak to you in terms you can appreciate and understand. Communication between doctor and patient is very important, but with fifteen to thirty minutes or even longer of doctor's office visits, a lot of specific details can still get lost or passed over. Through my own journey of finding answers, I have learned more about the digestive system than I ever thought I wanted to know. I have also learned how important it is for patients to ask as many questions as they need in order to feel comfortable and to understand the details of their own health. It is crucial for doctors to explain systems, diagnoses, and test results with their patients, using terms the patient can understand and appreciate.

Being both doctor and patient, my engineering approach of collecting systematic information gave an advantage to find out answers that textbooks or doctors cannot give you directly. As a physician I had the proper tools and training to both self-diagnose and self-treat. Like anyone, I could search for answers to my symptoms on the Internet, but I could also apply my medical training, my critical thinking as a scientist, and my detailed knowledge of my own situation. I embarked on a journey of finding how to understand and treat my condition and finding the root cause of its symptoms. As I learned from my journey, symptoms are just the body's way of telling you there is something beneath the surface that needs to be addressed.

If we want to know what is happening at the point in the body where the symptoms are occurring, we need to take a good imaging *look* at it. An endoscope is a small tube with a tiny camera on one end that can enter a pathway such as the throat and esophagus into the stomach. With an upper-gastrointestinal (GI) endoscope to provide diagnostic help, I came away with some puzzles provided from the pathology report of an endoscopy. However, my pathway to success required more of an engineering pathway to find the working answers. (My physician only told me what "the finding" was but gave no explanation of the finding and no perspective on how it fit with normal or abnormal functioning.) He may have thought I could figure out the details with my own background as a physician.

With all of the engineering thinking, analysis, and trials of the treatment, I found the traditional medical concept approach was not working for me. Through systematic trials and record keeping, I finally found out how to control and to heal my symptoms, enabling me to enjoy life with a regular diet. I would like to share my own experience and my own engineering approach to develop ways to help others who also have GERD.

My major symptoms were stomach and intestinal burn at the same time following dinner or occasionally after a heavy brunch. The symptoms were relieved somewhat by over-the-counter antacids, but they were not a cure or a lasting solution. I also had symptoms of belching and of chest fullness after meals. I did have some reflux, but not as severe as when I had an *H. pylorus* infection (a bacterial digestive-tract infection) earlier that had been treated subsequently.

With many trials and analyses of individual symptoms, I finally systematically found ways to cure all of my symptoms. But this was not by way of traditional diagnosis and prescription drug treatment. I am certainly not against the pharmaceutical treatment that continues to benefit many patients. In my wish for an ideal situation for all, I would like every patient and their doctors to find exactly what the etiology of the patient's individual symptoms may be. I would like the doctor and the patient to communicate with each other better; establish a dialogue in plain language, not a pronouncement or a "lecture" from the doctor in technical terms.

Through much research, trial, and error, I found the answers that helped me cure my own condition. If I have one wish for this book, it is to share all of the information I have learned through both research and experience, in order to help anyone—patients and doctors alike—gain a better understanding of what is easily one of the most commonly diagnosed diseases in the United States today.

During the initial period of having GERD symptoms, I first turned to over-the-counter treatments, which proved to be "Band-Aids" at best for a condition that was both chronic and systemic. As a physician I found my situation to be both unique and frustrating because I realized that the treatment I might suggest for a patient suffering from symptoms similar to my own was not effective when I tried to treat myself.

I learned in medical school and medical practice how to diagnose by taking a history of the illness, including chief complaints, noting the duration of the symptoms and how such symptoms occurred, what (if any) associated symptoms might be, as well as what tends to aggravate or alleviate those symptoms. All of this, coupled with a clinical examination, usually allows a physician to arrive at a pointed diagnosis. If there is any doubt about the diagnosis, the doctor will make differential diagnosis by prescribing tests, observing the symptoms over time, or suggesting trials of treatment. This is systematic and makes sense.

For example, in my role as a neurologist, if you come to me complaining of headaches, I will ask the duration, the location, and the nature of the headaches; associated symptoms; frequency of the symptoms; and "trigger" factors you might be aware of, as well as previous trials of treatments. Typically, answering these questions after a clinical examination, it is not difficult for a doctor to make a diagnosis.

Most doctors tell patients what their diagnosis might be and what treatment plan is advisable. But not every doctor will discuss the etiology (the cause or origins of the symptoms) and treat the root cause of the disease, rather than just treating symptoms. Many doctors take a "treat first" approach, having the patient leave with a prescription for medications to control symptoms, but leaving with little understanding of his or her own condition.

My own clinical symptoms seemed easy to diagnose at first, but as they persisted, a differential diagnosis was difficult without further diagnostic testing. Not wanting to take time out of my busy schedule, I decided against scheduling a diagnostic test, in this case endoscopy, and instead diagnosed myself without a clear etiology (i.e., root cause). I decided that the best thing would be trials of treatment. But when all of the methods I would typically prescribe for my own patients failed, I turned to natural treatments. Instead of just watching *what* I ate, I also began to watch *how much* I ate and *when* I ate it. This was more of an "engineering" approach, with systematic record keeping. I was now studying the behaviors and factors and timing of the system I wanted to improve upon. I was behaving more like an engineer solving a problem and less like a traditional physician trying to eliminate a symptom. When I finally did have an endoscopy, the results showed that I did not have a malignancy. I realized the one thing I had yet to try was to help boost and heal the very system that was giving me trouble. I needed to find a way to help my digestive system function more optimally. This became a paradox—as I tried to help myself using conventional treatments of antibiotics for bronchitis and proton-pump inhibitors to ease my reflux, I was actually just adding to my own problem.

Chapter 1

Do I Have GERD?

Just about everybody gets an occasional upset stomach, whether from sensitivity to spicy foods or from overeating (Rees 1997). I had occasionally suffered from minor upset stomach until August 2012. In May of that year, I had returned from a trip to San Francisco, where the weather was chilly. (San Francisco gets the most fog in the warmer months.) On the plane ride home, I was sitting near a child who coughed for the duration of the six-hour flight. It was no surprise to me that I came down with a viral bronchial infection once I returned home to the East Coast. For two and a half months, I suffered from a terrible cough. I tried antibiotics, but none of them helped me completely, as the initial illness was viral in nature; antibiotics fight and kill bacteria. Finally I decided to try a low dose of steroid medication, and eventually the cough stopped.

Once the cough cleared, I gradually began to feel some indigestion and strange gastrointestinal symptoms. The symptoms occurred primarily after dinner. I felt general discomfort—fullness and terrible reflux—and then the reflux caused my coughing to return. After dinner I would feel congested; sometimes I would wheeze, and my stomach would burn—not in my esophagus, as is normally associated with heartburn, but lower and off to the side in my actual stomach. Sometimes I would feel abdominal burning or a cold sensation. Then I sometimes experienced dysphagia (difficulty swallowing) for solid foods like bread, which had happened rarely in the past. Sometimes eating fruit or spicy food or even the littlest bit of butter or oil would make my stomach burn right away.

I am a neurologist by training, so the nuances of the digestive system were outside my area of expertise. I needed help, but putting myself in the hands of a fellow physician wasn't easy. Not only are doctors notoriously bad patients, but many of us are on a very tight schedule that makes it difficult for us to make time for our own personal exams and diagnostic testing. In Chinese culture, the eagle represents strength, the hero. We have a saying: "The self eagle sometimes creates the problem." In this instance,

I felt I had no choice but to make the definite decision to fully become a patient myself.

When I first had my own GI symptoms, I was not worried. But when the symptoms did not go away, I grew concerned. I realized that my two previous treating physicians for my *H. Pylori* were happy to treat me but didn't tell me the cause or prognosis (the likely future of the symptoms) to indicate that there could be a lingering effect. I learned at this point that I needed to tell *my* patients what they should be looking for all along the way—both during and after treatment of their individual disorders. If the doctor and the patient open up clear lines of communication with each other, a lot of learning can take place for both.

As a physician, I diagnosed myself with GERD; however, GERD is really a symptom or the core expression of several different diseases. GERD's major symptoms are reflux and heartburn. Given that my symptoms extended beyond those common core symptoms, I needed a more complete diagnosis. I knew then that an endoscopy would provide more answers, but that would cost me my tightly scheduled time, so I decided to do trials of treatment first. I wanted to learn as much as I could about the disease.

When people hear the term GERD, they most often think "heartburn," and heartburn can be a component of the disease. But GERD is actually a systemic affliction of the digestive tract that over 60 percent of the population in the United States will report suffering as a symptom at some point in any given calendar year. As much as 20 percent of the population will report suffering symptoms weekly, if not daily (Amos 2012). With statistics like these, it is no surprise that a noticeable percentage of my neurology patients have complained of GI reflux symptoms or that a high percentage of my patients are already taking antacid prescription medications.

What Is GERD?

GERD is not just occasional heartburn. Heartburn is a feeling of pressure or burning pain behind the breastbone that many people suffer after eating a large meal or certain trigger foods, such as spicy or highly acidic foods. GERD is caused by a regular occurrence of heartburn or reflux or the backup of stomach contents (refluxate stomach acid, bile, pepsin, or pancreatic enzymes) into the esophagus (Mayo Clinic Staff 2016).

When a person who does not have GERD swallows, the lower esophageal sphincter—a band of muscle around the lower part of the esophagus (at the top of the stomach)—relaxes, allowing food and drink to flow down into the stomach before closing again. In order for this to happen, the normal pressure of the lower esophageal sphincter (LES) must exceed gastric pressure inside the stomach that exerts pressure back upward. Any acid remaining in the esophagus is then neutralized with bicarbonate, a substance found in our saliva. LES pressure is generally lowest in the daytime after a meal and highest at night. This situation prevents stomach contents from going back up into the esophagus. Relaxation of the LES happens a few times per day in unafflicted people, and it is unclear why this relaxation happens more frequently in people with GERD ("Gastroesophageal Reflux Disease" 2016).

A person with GERD experiences a regular malfunction of the lower esophageal sphincter, in which it either relaxes or it has become weakened and allows stomach contents to flow back into the esophagus. This is what causes the sensation of heartburn. The esophageal lining isn't resistant to hydrochloric acid in the same way that the lining of the stomach is; therefore, the esophagus is easily injured from exposure to acid over time and accounts for much of the discomfort one feels from GERD.

Possible Etiology of GERD

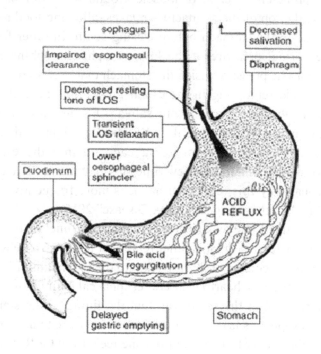

TABLE 2
Substances that influence lower esophageal sphincter pressure (LESP)

	Increase LESP	Decrease LESP
Hormones	Gastrin, motilin, substance P	Secretin, cholecystokinin, glucagon, gastric inhibitory polypeptide, vasoactive intestinal polypeptide, progesterone
Neural agents	Alpha-adrenergic agonists, beta-adrenergic antagonists, cholinergic agonists	Alpha-adrenergic antagonists, beta-adrenergic agonists, cholinergic antagonists, serotonin
Medications	Metoclopramide, domperidone, prostaglandin $F_{2\alpha}$, cisapride	Nitrates, calcium channel blockers, theophylline, morphine, meperidine, diazepam, barbiturates
Foods	Protein	Fat, chocolate, ethanol, peppermint

Reprinted from reference 13 with permission from Elsevier.

Factors that can contribute to the development of GERD are alcohol use, pregnancy, smoking, and being overweight. Regular consumption of certain foods can also contribute to the development of GERD, such as citrus fruits, chocolate (which can relax the LES), caffeinated drinks, fried or fatty foods, onions and garlic, mint flavorings, spicy foods, spaghetti sauce, pizza, chili, or other tomato-based foods. Alcohol can lead to a temporary weakening of the LES, allowing one to experience GERD (Mayo Clinic Staff 2016).

Other factors include a person's inability to clear acid from the esophagus by means of peristalsis (the waves of contraction and relaxation of smooth muscle that move food through the stomach and digestive system), inability to produce adequate saliva ("dry mouth"), and inadequate tissue resistance to hydrochloric acid. Over time, this process can lead to the erosion of the esophageal lining and stomach lining, causing further complications from the disease ("Gastroesophageal Reflux Disease" 2016).

A doctor can diagnose GERD either via symptoms reported by a patient or, upon examination, by noting esophageal damage caused by reflux over time.

Types of GERD

Symptomatic GERD: Burning sensation in the chest or throat; stomach contents coming back up into the throat or mouth; sour, acid, or bitter taste in the mouth.

Nighttime GERD: Nighttime awakening due to symptoms such as coughing or choking from stomach contents coming up into the throat; sour, acid, or bitter taste in the mouth; pieces of food in the throat. General GERD symptoms appear when lying down and/or upon waking up in the morning. Patients with nighttime GERD tend to have a lower quality of life because of complications such as sleep disruption (Lowe 2006).

Some degree of reflux is normal, especially after a large meal. This reflux is typically counterbalanced by peristalsis (the natural, rhythmic movement of food through the digestive system), gravity (which is why many people suffer from reflux when lying down), and neutralization of acid by saliva. When one or more of these mechanisms don't function well enough to allow refluxed material to move back down into the stomach, GERD symptoms can occur.

People who experience GERD might have decreased LES resting tone and/or increased TLESRs. TLESRs, or transient lower esophageal sphincter relaxations, are relaxations of the LES that occur even without food intake, in order to cause LES pressure to remain equal to gastric pressures. They generally last around ten to thirty seconds, during which time reflux can occur. This is the most common cause of GERD. Decreased resting LES tone or a weak LES will cause stomach pressure to exceed LES pressure. This is most commonly seen in people with severe GERD (Lowe 2006). Other factors contribute to GERD.

Impaired esophageal acid clearance is an inability to clear acid from the esophagus, which can be caused by impaired peristalsis and/or inadequate amounts of saliva following peristalsis. Impaired esophageal acid clearance is commonly found in those who suffer from GERD related to hiatal hernia ("Gastroesophageal Reflux Disease" 2016).

Delayed gastric emptying, also called "gastroparesis," is a disorder that slows or stops the movement of food from the stomach to the small intestine. Stomach muscles are controlled by the vagus nerve, and typically those muscles contract to break up food and move it through the gastrointestinal tract. Delayed gastric emptying can occur when the vagus nerve has been damaged, stopping the stomach muscles from functioning normally. Food then moves at a much slower rate from the stomach to the small intestine or stops moving altogether. The most common cause of gastroparesis is diabetes because high blood glucose levels can damage the vagus nerve over time. The vagus nerve is a large, long nerve that controls the LES and many other bodily functions selectively. Other causes could be Parkinson's disease, multiple sclerosis, or damage caused during intestinal surgery (Lowe 2006).

Common symptoms include nausea, bloating, stomach pain, feeling full even after eating only a small meal, loss of appetite, and regurgitating undigested food (Mayo Clinic Staff 2016).

Decreased salivation, also known as sialoschesis, is most commonly a side effect of various medications. More than five hundred different prescription drugs list dry mouth as a side effect. A more obvious cause would be chronic dehydration due to inadequate fluid intake, excessive sweating, vomiting, or diarrhea. It takes about 7 ml of saliva to neutralize 1 ml of hydrochloric acid. Salivation slows to the point of almost stopping during sleep, severely impairing the mechanism of esophageal acid clearance just prior to or during sleep (Lowe 2006).

Impaired tissue resistance is caused when the esophageal lining, or mucosa, is unable to withstand injury from contact with refluxate. Age and diet seem to play a role in maintaining a proper esophageal barrier to prevent tissue injury. Normally the esophagus produces protective and neutralizing substances (namely mucus and bicarbonate) in order to prevent injury. Damage occurs when the level of pepsin and acid in the refluxate becomes higher than what the mucosal lining can withstand (Lowe 2006).

A defect in any one of these mechanisms can lead to GERD-like symptoms, as can any condition that increases intragastric pressure, such as obesity, pregnancy, or a hiatal hernia, which reduces LES pressure due to displacement of the LES segment of the esophagus. This leads to a diminished ability to clear acid from the esophagus.

Symptoms of GERD
heartburn
regurgitation of food or bitter-tasting liquid
trouble swallowing (dysphagia)
pain with swallowing, hoarseness, sore throat
increased salivation (also known as water brash)
nausea
chest pain
chronic cough
asthma
erosion of dental enamel
dentine hypersensitivity
sinusitis and damaged teeth
sensation of a lump in the throat

I had stomach burning, which could be gastritis. But why did it only happen after dinner? It did not happen after breakfast or lunch each day. My indigestion could be a part of gastritis, and my reflux symptoms could be gastroesophageal reflux disease. But why would I have symptoms in my stomach and abdomen simultaneously, even when food had not traveled there yet?

Upon self-examination of my symptoms, I realized I only have the two most common: heartburn or stomach burn and mild dysphagia. I had experienced the less-common symptoms of reflux laryngitis and sinusitis, but those symptoms had passed. I knew I had GERD but was uncertain of the etiology without tissue sampling and pathology diagnosis. The most common etiology is dysfunction or loosened-tone lower esophagus sphincter (LES). If I had dysfunction of the LES, surely I would have reflux and probably chest congestion. However, what caused the other symptoms—simultaneously having abdominal coldness, intestinal burning sensation, and indigestion?

Answer Number One

I had suffered from an infection of *Helicobacter pylori* in the past. I knew I might be suffering from gastritis due to that infection or from chronic gastritis, with which I had been diagnosed twelve years before. But why would symptoms occur now, after the infection had been cleared for so long?

I know that all too often doctors do not answer all the questions patients have about their symptoms. Here I was, trying to answer my own questions as both doctor and patient, and I realized I could not. Why did I have so much discomfort after meals? Why did I feel so full, even after a small meal? Why only at dinner?

The term *dyspepsia* often comes up in association with GERD, so I decided I needed to learn more about that condition. Dyspepsia, synonymous with indigestion, is a condition wherein digestion is impaired. Symptoms include abdominal fullness and/or feeling fuller than expected after eating even a small meal, chronic pain in the upper abdomen, nausea, belching, and heartburn (Bazaldua 1999).

I didn't have all the symptoms of dyspepsia, but I realized that some of the symptoms fit absolutely. After my mother passed away in 2009, I went through an understandable period of depression. Soon after, I experienced decreased appetite, a feeling of fullness after dinner, some belching, and weight loss. But a diagnosis of dyspepsia does not give answers as to why my symptoms were occurring and why they were not going away.

Eventually I arrived at the possibility that I might have stomach cancer. My chances are increased because I am Asian and because I have been previously infected with *H. pylori*. The symptoms seemed to fit: indigestion and stomach discomfort, a bloated feeling after eating, loss of appetite, and heartburn. My anxiety increased with the possibility of a malignancy, but otherwise my mental and physical condition seemed good. So I tried to convince myself that there had to be another explanation by finding the cause of each of my several symptoms.

In an engineering approach to problem solving, one must first understand the individual parts of the system and their relationships in the system one is trying to change. I made a complete list of my symptoms. Alongside each I wrote notes about the behavior and timing of that symptom.

Reflux is caused by LES dysfunction, which could have been caused by gastritis and the *H. Pylori* infection that I was treated for in 1999. Just to be certain that I was not suffering reinfection, I took a breathing test for *H. Pylori* again. The results came out negative. With that ruled out, I became even more puzzled.

What was causing the simultaneous hot and cold sensations in my abdomen right after dinner? I did know those symptoms happened after I used antibiotics for two weeks when I had suffered a two-month period of coughing. Also, the steroids I used to treat my cough turned out to be a bad choice overall. This is because a side effect of using steroids is that they increase the production of stomach acid while they decrease the production of protective mucus. This combination was a likely culprit in irritating the lining of my stomach but did not account for the extreme feeling of fullness I was experiencing after dinner.

One of the potential causes of GERD is a hiatal hernia. The majority of patients with hiatal hernia, particularly a type-1 hiatal hernia (also known as a sliding hiatal hernia), have no symptoms. My symptoms were not totally consistent with this diagnosis but could potentially contribute to one of the etiologies ("Hiatal Hernia Causes and Symptoms" 2015).

The next potential cause could be alcohol abuse or pregnancy; I had neither. I do not drink alcohol. I am not obese; my BMI (body mass index) was only slightly above normal but not to the point of cause or concern. The only thing I could think of was that food was causing the problem.

As I learned, the other contributor to GERD includes delayed gastric emptying because of weakness of the vagus nerve in Parkinson's patients and diabetes patients. It seemed not to apply to me. (The vagus controls the closing of the LES at the top of the stomach and the opening of the pyloric sphincter at the bottom of the stomach.)

Trial One of Treatment: Diet Control

At this time, I only chose "trials of treatment" to treat the symptoms. Common sense tells you that if you eat something and it makes you uncomfortable, you should avoid it in the future. Since my symptoms were mostly occurring after dinner, I examined what I ate regularly with that meal. Maybe bread was the problem, as I couldn't imagine the ground turkey and fresh vegetables I ate regularly would cause this much upset, if any at all. I switched my bread at dinner from white to whole wheat, and that seemed to lend some improvement. I also modified my diet to exclude acidic foods—citrus, tomatoes, also spicy foods, chocolate, dairy, or wine (which I rarely drank and in very tiny portions if at all). I began to feel more and more improvement, particularly during the weekdays after breakfast and lunch. But I still experienced my symptom of stomach burning on the weekends. Why?

I examined my routines (I am a creature of habit) and realized that on weekends I don't have the same lunch that I do when I'm working in New York City during the week. Typically during the week I order food for lunch from a Chinese restaurant. On the weekends, my husband and I go out to eat, and the things I like to order oftentimes have some dairy products.

My husband suggested coconut juice, which I considered. I had been paying attention to which foods were alkaline and which foods were acidic, but what I realized is that if you eat too much alkaline food, that stimulates more acid secretion in your body, which would only exacerbate my problem. I realized that the key was to maintain a healthy pH balance in my body. A balanced pH (an acid-alkaline balance) in your body fluids can make all the difference between high-quality health and multiple health issues. Coconut water is as close as you can get to the perfect pH for your internal fluids.

Bodies tend to be more acidic than alkaline. When you consume acidic foods and beverages, this can overtax your body's internal neutralizing system. Many pathogenic organisms (such as candida, bad bacteria) thrive in an acidic environment (Richlen 2008). An overgrowth of these pathogenic mircoforms can cause an overall toxic internal environment (as they steal nutrients and create toxic acids). This can lead to fatigue, weight gain, digestive issues, and a host of other serious health issues (Cowan 2016).

Coconut water alone did not work as a cure-all for me, so I continued on my pH-balancing quest by learning further about which foods would help me achieve balance.

Acid-Forming Foods and Beverages		
alcohol	asparagus	beans
brussels sprouts	cocoa	coffee

cornstarch	eggs	fish
flours and products	lentils	meat
mustard	noodles	oatmeal
olives	pastas	pepper
plums	poultry	prunes
shellfish	soft drinks	sugar
tea	vinegar	

Alkaline-Forming Foods		
avocados	corn	dates
fresh coconut	fresh fruits	most fresh vegetables
honey	horseradish	maple syrup
mushroom	onions	raisins
soy products	sprouts	

Willing to try anything, I tried an over-the-counter homeopathic remedy—orange-peel extract in capsule form that came highly recommended to me. It was very strong but did not work in my case.

I read recommendations such as using bromelain, an enzyme found in pineapple juice and pineapple stems, after meals. I read a suggestion that chewing gum to increase saliva production to neutralize acid in the esophagus might help, but my symptoms reached far beyond simple heartburn. One recommendation surprised me, which was to use melatonin, three to six milligrams per night, in order to help treat GERD. Most people know melatonin as an occasional sleep aid (for which recommended dosage is somewhere around 0.3 mg per night). What most people don't know is that melatonin is a powerful antioxidant (Kandil 2010).

Trial Two of Treatment—Over-the-Counter Antacids

When I focused on modifying my diet, I only experienced partial relief. It made sense that I could just have lingering gastritis from steroid use, so I decided to treat myself for gastritis by taking some over-the-counter antacid medication. My husband loves Maalox, which is a combination of aluminum hydroxide and magnesium hydroxide. These two ingredients neutralize excess acid produced by the stomach, which might offer me some relief. The drugstore nearest my house was out of Maalox, so my option was Gaviscon. It was very efficient. If I took one, even just once or twice a week, I found I felt pretty good all week, but certainly nowhere near what I used to consider normal. I refused to accept this state as "the new normal."

Gaviscon, like Maalox, contains aluminum hydroxide, which can be harmful to brain function if you consume too much. My husband bought me some Tums, which is calcium carbonate. The recommended dose to reduce acid was 1,500 mg. It was not as efficient as Gaviscon, and I didn't like the risk for kidney stones that came with taking a calcium carbonate-based antacid. Plus, taking something habitually to relieve the symptoms bothered me. I just wanted to be normal again. I knew the gastritis needed time to heal, but I was growing frustrated.

My daughter, who was a third-year medical-school student at the time, strongly suggested I have an endoscopy, and my husband agreed. This symptom cluster had been going on for too long, and they were all worried about me.

My thinking was that the endoscopy might confirm that I had gastritis or an ulcer. The worst-case scenario would be a cancer diagnosis. The diagnosis would change the treatment plan. I thought I would still try over-the-counter (OTC) antacid once a week and pay attention to my diet to let the gastritis heal.

Trial Three of Treatment: Pharmaceutical PPI (Proton-Pump Inhibitor)

Since I was still resistant to getting an endoscopy, my daughter suggested I start taking a proton-pump inhibitor such as Prilosec, Pepcid, or Zantac. Proton-pump inhibitors work by creating a long-term decrease in the production of stomach-acid secretion. Many people believe that GERD is due to an overproduction of stomach acid. This is simply not true, particularly as people age.

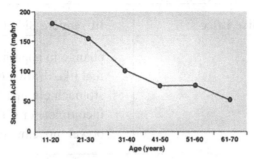

Fig. 1. Contrary to popular belief, stomach acid secretion tends to decline with advancing age. This graphs shows mean stomach acid secretion from the second decade to the eighth decade. (From "*Why Stomach Acid is Good For You.*")

If it were true, then why do people tend to suffer from GERD as they get older, when their levels of stomach acid have theoretically declined, rather than when they are younger and their stomach acid levels are at their highest? Some studies actually suggest that GERD results from stomach-acid levels being too low (Kresser 2010)!

I knew if I ate some citrus fruit or "citrated" food, that would worsen my symptoms, so I ignored this possibility.

Prevacid seemed to help me twelve years ago, when I had *H. Pylori* treatment, so I decided to give it a try again. I began to take it every night. The first day I felt less stomach burning. I then noticed a significant decrease in appetite. After four to five days, my symptoms were worse in terms of congestion after dinner, and the feeling of fullness was back in force, as was the burning. The worst thing was that I could not lie down. Every time I went to lie down, I would have terrible coughing that kept me up all night.

I tried eating dinner earlier and took up after-dinner walking. I also changed my bread to gluten free. I slept with two pillows to prop me upright until 2:00 a.m., and I would sleep from 2:00 a.m. to 7:00 a.m. It was just enough for me to maintain my busy patient-care schedule. I began to lose weight and noticed a significant decrease in stool volume.

It just didn't seem possible that suddenly my GERD would worsen at the same time I started taking Prevacid. The only explanation was that I was experiencing severe side effects from the medication. I began researching the side effects of the drug, Lansoprazole. The list was extensive!

Common Side Effects:	Infrequent Side Effects:
itching rash diarrhea dizziness head pain	change in appetite feel like throwing up stomach cramps incomplete or infrequent bowel movements

Rare Side Effects:	
Severe	Less Severe
depression increased pressure in eyes cataracts abnormal heart rhythm acute infection of the nose, throat, or sinus allergies affecting the sinuses, nose, or throat lung fibrosis\ ulcerated colon hepatitis caused by drugs gallstones acute inflammation of the pancreas interstitial nephritis severe bloody diarrhea from antibiotics erythema multiforme toxic epidermal necrolysis Stevens-Johnson syndrome muscle pain flulike symptoms cough inability to empty bladder	problem emptying stomach contents ringing in the ears painful, red, or swollen mouth mouth irritation painful, red, or swollen tongue disorder of the anus or rectum bursitis muscle inflammation sensation of spinning or whirling

candida infection	fever
broken bone	pain
life-threatening allergic	chills
reaction	taste problems
hemolytic anemia	visible water retention
decrease of all cells in the	swollen lymph nodes
blood	vomiting
bone-marrow failure	gas
low platelet count and	swelling of the abdomen
bleeding from immune	numbness and tingling
response	feeling weak
decreased blood platelets	low amount of magnesium in
deficiency of granulocytes	the blood
decreased white blood cells	anemia[1]
decreased neutrophils	
anxiety	

Nowhere in the listed side effects was the worsening of reflux. My only side effects on these lists were decreased appetite and decreased stool volume. I was overwhelmed by the side effect of the Prevacid. I did not pay attention the one side effect of "problem emptying stomach contents" that acutely caused all of my symptoms, in retrospect. Nevertheless, I decided to stop the Prevacid. It did not work for me now the way it did when I used it to treat my HP infections. For whatever reason, this time around it made my symptoms worse. I had no explanation. Two days after stopping Prevacid, I was able to sleep without having to prop myself up.

Trial Four of Treatment: Natural Products Healing Heartburn

As conventional methods had not helped me, I decided to turn to natural ways of healing myself. My husband is a biochemist; he suggested I try to create my own internal antacid by eating more alkaline foods. One day he brought home artichoke extract which, aside from having very high antioxidant capacity, has high levels of a chemical called cynarin, which stimulates the flow of bile from the liver (Cutler 2011).

---

[1]   "Lansoprazole Side Effects in Detail" 2016.

Bile is a fluid produced by the liver that helps break down fats in the small intestine. Bile increases the absorption of fats, therefore increasing the absorption of fat-soluble vitamins such as A, D, E, and K. The liver continually produces bile, which is then stored in the gall bladder until you eat, at which time it is released into the duodenum. Since bile is alkaline, it helps neutralize excess stomach acid, which not only helps reduce acid reflux but also helps neutralize stomach contents in preparation for digestive enzymes, which work best in alkaline conditions (*Encyclopædia Britannica* 2016).

Since it is supposed to help with dyspepsia, I decided to try artichoke. I didn't even have time to notice any benefit, because I experienced immediate insomnia after taking the extract. The major components of artichoke extract are cynarin and chlorogenic acids. Chlorogenic acids are one component of both green tea and coffee that make them mild stimulants. Taking artichoke extract later in the day (after dinner), as I did, can lead to shallow sleep or outright insomnia.

Artichoke extract is wonderful for a host of other health benefits. Not only does it increase bile flow, but it can help to reduce nausea, has fantastic antioxidant properties, and has been shown to lower cholesterol and triglycerides. Nevertheless, I had to stop taking it.

I tried some manuka honey, as my doctor suggested, but I felt no significant effect. Then I tried fresh coconut water; sometimes it seemed to work, but other times it seemed to make things worse. I grew more and more dejected. I followed a diet, avoiding acidic foods, but I felt as though I was just keeping symptoms at bay, rather than actually curing what was wrong with me. I began to grow more anxious that something might really be wrong with me.

It has long been thought that melatonin is solely the product of the pineal gland in the brain, but recent research has shown that melatonin is present in multiple body systems, including the digestive tract, suggesting that it serves a function in digestive processes.

Researchers have studied the effects of melatonin in the treatment of GERD, both on its own and in conjunction with a PPI. What they found is that over a four-week period, patients treated with melatonin in conjunction with a PPI experienced complete remission of their GERD symptoms, compared to patients who were treated with just a PPI on its own. What they also found was that patients treated with *only* melatonin for eight weeks experienced the same remission.

Unlike PPIs, melatonin can be taken at relatively high doses with very little or no toxicity. Melatonin, taken in a 3–6 mg dose at bedtime, produces far fewer side effects than PPI medications. The role of melatonin in treating GERD is threefold. First, melatonin is a powerful free-radical scavenger and protects mucosal tissue from oxidative damage. Second, melatonin also has a significant positive impact on lower esophageal sphincter function, possibly due to its inhibitory effect on gastric-acid secretion and gastrin release, which stimulates esophageal-sphincter contraction. Third, melatonin is believed to prevent esophageal damage from GERD by increasing blood flow and anti-inflammatory molecules in esophageal mucus. Additionally, melatonin provides all of these protective benefits without lowering overall gastric acidity like PPIs are designed to do, which cause many of the adverse side effects from taking PPI medication.

In less severe cases, treatment with melatonin over an eight-week period yields promising results. In more severe cases, co-treatment with melatonin and a lower dose of PPI medication may provide complete relief with fewer side effects than PPI treatment alone (Kandil 2010).

After I learned all the benefits of melatonin, I just did not want to try it. Being a neurologist, I was concerned about the biologic feedback from taking "extra melatonin" that could suppress the body's natural rate of secretion of melatonin (negative feedback) by long- term use of the exogenous neurohormone.

In 2001 and again in 2006, William Yancy of Duke University and his colleagues published results from two studies that showed that an extremely low-carbohydrate diet vastly improves GERD.

In the first study they enrolled five patients with GERD who had all failed to recover using conventional treatments. Within one week of starting a very low-carbohydrate (VLC) diet, while some of the patients continued to use GERD-unfriendly substances such as caffeine and alcohol, all symptoms were resolved.

In the second study he enrolled eight obese participants who suffered from extreme GERD and used the Johnson-DeMeester test to measure how much acid was backing up into the esophagus. Five of the eight participants had abnormal Johnson-DeMeester scores (high levels of acid in the esophagus) at the beginning of the trial, but after adopting a VLC diet, their scores lowered to the range that would be expected were they on PPI treatment. It should be noted that obesity is, in and of itself, a risk factor for GERD, as an increased BMI creates intraabdominal pressure, which causes dysfunction of the LES. A VLC diet is likely to promote weight loss and could very well have been a partial factor in the results of the second study.

All eight subjects in the 2006 study reported a vast reduction in their GERD symptoms, which shows that there is both subjective and objective evidence to support a VLC diet as a treatment method for GERD.

I did not try the VLC diet until later. It is very effective. Please see the chapter on enzymes.

By this point, after two months of the symptoms, monitoring my PH, and eating a low-carbohydrate diet, my reflux was livable. I still suffered some dysphagia, but it, along with my cough, was improving. Yet the symptoms were still there in the background. I felt my digestive health was like the weather. Every morning I would wake up and hope for a "sunny" day, but it was never consistent. Some days were sunny, but some days were cloudy, and others brought rain where my symptoms were concerned.

One of my patients reported to me that she had been diagnosed with stomach cancer two years ago, had surgery with chemotherapy, and now everything seemed fine. I couldn't help but wonder if that was what was wrong with me.

Chapter 2

Do I Need to Treat H. Pylori?

Since I had tried every method I could think of to cure myself of GERD and was unsuccessful, I had to seek more answers. As a doctor, the next differential diagnosis I would make for my patient would be chronic gastritis with acute exacerbation. However, there was no abdominal pain to support such a diagnosis. Indigestion is part of gastritis, and that can be caused by past infection of *H. pylori*, which I had and for which I was treated. A recent breathing test was negative for a recurrence of *H. pylori*, but I wondered if maybe there was a lingering effect.

My overall health is very good, but I've experienced mild GI symptoms on and off for my whole adult life. My first heartburn symptoms started when I was twenty years old. That year my parents moved to a southern province in China, where tangerines were a popular crop. My mother shipped me a large bucket of tangerines, approximately thirty pounds! They were delicious. I ate five to ten of them a day. After a week, I felt a burning sensation in my stomach. I realized that some foods, no matter how good (or how good for you) can also cause problems.

For my entire adult life, I haven't had much problem with my stomach except for occasional mild pain in my upper-left-quadrant area, which is where the large curve of the stomach is. It only happens if I have eaten too much or eaten acidic or spicy food. It had never been a big deal. Everyone has a tummy ache from time to time.

In 1999 I began experiencing some acid reflux in my throat. I also lost a significant amount of weight, down to 109 pounds from 125 pounds. At the time I was very busy with my medical practice, but I felt healthy overall, so I did not pay attention to it. I was a part of a group practice at the time, so it was convenient to ask one of my colleagues that I most trusted about my symptoms. She suggested I check for *H. pylori*, a bacterium that can cause the symptoms I was experiencing. She arranged a blood test for me, and there were very high titers (concentration) in my blood.

I immediately had an appointment with my primary-care physician, who had been my attending-physician mentor when I was intern in New

York University (Langone) Tisch Hospital. He told me what I needed to know.

What Is H. Pylori?

H. pylori is a Gram-negative bacterial pathogen. *Helicobacter pylori*, a bacterium commonly found in the stomach, selectively colonizes the gastric epithelium. It infects approximately one half of the world's population. Most infected people never experience any symptoms, but *H. pylori* is capable of causing a host of digestive issues including gastritis, ulcers, and rarely, stomach cancer (Mayo Clinic Staff 2014).

According to the National Institutes of Health, approximately 20 percent of people under forty years old and 50 percent of adults over sixty in the United States are infected. Rates of infection are higher in developing countries.

Cause of Infection?

H. pylori is thought to spread by consuming food or water contaminated with fecal matter and possibly through oral transmission via saliva. The bacterium is more prevalent in institutionalized children, families, or people who live in generally close contact (Mayo Clinic Staff 2014).

H. pylori causes changes to the stomach and duodenum (the first part of the small intestine). The bacteria infect the protective lining of the stomach, causing inflammation, which leads to the release of certain enzymes and a cytotoxin called Vac-A that then trigger the immune system. These processes may injure the cells of the stomach or duodenum, causing inflammation in the walls of the stomach (gastritis) or duodenum (duodenitis). Research has shown that stomach acid stimulates *H. pylori*, which furthers colonization and therefore inflammation and formation of ulcers (Starpoli 2015).

GERD has always been thought to occur independently of *H. pylori* infection because, in studies, *H. pylori* infection occurred at a similar rate in people afflicted with GERD as it did in control groups. More recently, however, it has been suggested that *H. pylori* might have a protective effect against GERD, as *H. Pylori*-induced inflammation of the stomach lining actually *reduces* acid secretion, therefore diminishing the acidic potency of the refluxate. Scientists made repeated observations of the emergence of

GERD in some patients after *H. pylori* eradication and also observed a low incidence of *H. pylori* infection among GERD patients. There is, however, no direct causative effect of *H. pylori* eradication and the development of GERD, so the decision to treat *H. pylori* should be made between doctor and patient (Richter 2004).

What Causes H. Pylori *Infection?*

According to Dr. Martin Blaser, humans and *H. pylori* have been coevolving for thousands of years, and, until quite recently, everyone was colonized by the bacteria. So if *H. pylori* was part of our normal gut flora, why is colonization by the bacteria now considered an infection?

When the environment of the microorganism is altered, changes can occur in the relationship between host and pathogen, and illness can arise. It is also possible for an asymptomatic host to infect another person, who could then develop disease as a result of infection while the host remains asymptomatic.

Certain factors can cause this relationship to change, or the introduction of a competing microorganism can cause the preexisting microorganism to become more virulent.

When the relationship between host and *H. pylori* becomes noncommensal, the stomach increases production of gastrin, which causes parietal cells to increase the amount of acid they secrete. The increase of acid and pepsin can cause the stomach lining to erode, which can lead to the formation of a peptic or duodenal ulcer. Fifteen percent of people infected with *H. pylori* will develop an ulcer. Other clinical manifestations of *H. pylori* include chronic gastritis and atrophic gastritis (which, over time, causes a decrease in stomach-acid output) and stomach cancer. When a decrease in stomach acid and damage to parietal cells (which produce intrinsic factor) occurs, *H. Pylori* infections can lead to arthritis (mainly calcification and spurs), anemia, and vitamin B12 deficiency.

Dr. Martin Blaser, a microbiologist at New York University School of Medicine, has made a career of understanding *H. pylori* and our tumultuous relationship with it. *H. pylori* not only helps regulate stomach acid, but it also serves an anti-inflammatory function, which may explain why populations that peacefully coexist with *H. pylori* tend to have lower rates of allergy and asthma than we do in Western society. Blaser has also found evidence that *H. pylori* may serve a metabolic function, in that it helps regulate ghrelin, a hormone that signals the brain that we are hungry and it's time to eat. When we are full, our production of ghrelin shuts down. Eradicating *H. pylori* from our system may quiet those signals, which could, in turn, cause overeating. Is it possible that the epidemic of obesity in Western society could be due in part to the eradication of *H. pylori*?

Of course, our relationship with *H. pylori* is not a "marriage made in heaven." Most of the ills attributed to *H. pylori* appear later in life. If Blaser had his way, he would inoculate children with *H. pylori* so that they would enjoy all of the benefits of *H. pylori* for the first half of their life and then kill the bug at around age forty, to prevent what he feels is the bug's evolutionary purpose—to ultimately take us down in our later years (Hadley 2006).

Non-Digestive Conditions Associated with *H. Pylori*	
Vascular Diseases ischemic heart disease primary Raynaud's phenomenon primary headache arteriosclerosis atrial fibrillation Skin Diseases idiopathic chronic urticaria rosacea alopecia areata Autoimmune Diseases Sjogren's syndrome autoimmune thyroiditis autoimmune thrombocytopenia Schoenlein-Henoch purpura	Respiratory chronic bronchitis pulmonary tuberculosis bronchiectasis lung cancer bronchial asthma Other Diseases liver cirrhosis growth retardation chronic idiopathic sideropenia sudden infant death diabetes mellitus gum disease[2]

[2] "Helicobacter Pylori Related Diseases & Conditions", 2016.

Treatment of H. pylori

H. pylori is typically treated with antibiotics, often in conjunction with other agents. This treatment is highly effective but can cause side effects and antibiotic resistance. The most common and effective treatment currently involves two potent antibiotics (such as clarithromycin and metronidazole) twice per day, along with a proton pump inhibitor such as lansoprazole for seven days. Sometimes it is recommended that patients continue on PPI treatment for an additional two to four weeks, in order to help heal any existing ulcerations (Kusters 2006).

Treatment of *H. pylori* with probiotic therapy has shown encouraging results. Probiotics inhibit colonization and decrease gastric inflammation. Combination antibiotic/probiotic therapy increased eradication results by 10 percent in human studies. No study has shown eradication of *H. pylori* using just probiotic therapy, but long-term use of probiotics may be an effective way to keep infection at bay (Lesbros-Pantoflickova 2007).

Statistics have shown that children treated with antibiotics tend to have an increase in the development of asthma. Children treated with some specific antibiotics can develop hearing impairment. Children infected with *H. pylori*, however, tend to be 40 to 60 percent less likely to have childhood asthma. Unfortunately, the same statistic does not hold true for adults.

Some methods, used in conjunction with antibiotic therapy, have proved useful in helping to further eradication of infection and also to alleviate antibiotic side effects.

Probiotic Therapy

Probiotics are "gut-friendly" bacteria or microbes that have a positive impact on digestion. Improved digestion, in turn, improves overall health. The most commonly studied probiotics are those that produce lactic acid, particularly *Lactobacillus acidophilus* and *Bifidus*. Probiotics can assist in treatment for *H. pylori* infection by mitigating headaches, nausea, and general dyspepsia that can be associated with low stomach acid, but more importantly, by helping to inhibit the bug by producing antimicrobial substances and also by competing with *H. pylori* for adhesion to gastric epithelial cells. Adhesion is an important factor in *H. pylori* infection, as it prevents clearance of the bug via peristaltic activity, flow of liquid through the stomach, and shedding of the mucosal layer.

Probiotics may also inhibit *H. pylori* through the secretion of antibacterial substances, most commonly lactic and acetic acids and hydrogen peroxide, which occurs as a result of the fermentation of lactic acid (Lesbros-Pantoflickova 2007).

Bismuth

Bismuth, a heavy-metal compound, is an ingredient found in some over-the-counter antacid treatments such as Pepto-Bismol and can be used in conjunction with other *H. pylori* treatment methods. Bismuth, as a heavy metal, has a toxic effect on several types of microbes (Bland 2004).

Sulforaphane

When a cruciferous plant, such as broccoli, cauliflower, cabbage, kale, and brussels sprouts, is damaged (such as by chewing), the enzyme myrosinase transforms glucoraphanin, part of the defense mechanism of the plant, into raphanin (a natural antibiotic) and sulforaphane, a compound known for its anticancer and antimicrobial properties. Broccoli sprouts have thirty to fifty times the concentration of glucoraphanin compared to mature broccoli and have been shown to reduce *H. pylori* levels by up to 40 percent. The effect of sulforaphane has not, however, been shown to eradicate *H. pylori* (Haristoy 2003).

Extra-Virgin Pine Nut Oil (EVPO)

This oil has a long history of medicinal use in Russian and Chinese traditional medicine, particularly for digestive purposes. An excellent free-radical scavenger, EVPO helps to prevent and/or reverse oxidative stress that can lead to peptic ulcers and gastritis.

H. pylori contributes to oxidative stress by producing urease, an enzyme that neutralizes gastric acid by catalyzing urea, which in turn releases ammonia and carbon dioxide. An *H. pylori* infection causes the deployment of neutrophils (a particular type of white blood cell), which produce reactive oxygen species (ROS) that lead to the release free radicals, causing damage to the epithelium. The presence of urease is used in the diagnosis of *Helicobacter pylori*.

Extra-virgin pine nut oil can help heal conditions related to an inflammation of the gastrointestinal lining by helping to mitigate free-radical damage. Take one teaspoon thirty to sixty minutes before each meal; double that if you are trying to heal duodenal ulcers. The average user feels significant relief of symptoms within seven to ten days (Hart 2010).

Manuka Honey

Manuka honey is honey produced by bees that feed off of the nectar from the flowers of the Manuka bush (*Leptospermum scoparium*), native to New Zealand and southeast Australia.

In 1991 a study by Ali, et al. showed that regular honey had an inhibitory effect on the proliferation of *H. pylori* at solutions of 10 percent and 20 percent. Further studies showed that Manuka honey had an even more promising effect at concentrations of only 5 percent. While these statistics are promising in terms of relieving symptoms and inhibiting further proliferation of the bug, no honey has been shown to eradicate infection (Nzeako 2006).

It is uncertain why Manuka honey has a statistically more significant effect on the inhibitory effect of *H. pylori*, but it is something that definitely warrants further investigation.

Mastic

Mastic (also called arabic gum) comes from the resin of a tree (*Pistacia lentiscus*) and has been used in herbal medicine since ancient times. Hippocrates recommended mastic as a preventative remedy for digestive upset, a use for which it is still known today. Mastic gum has been shown as an effective inhibitor of *H. pylori*. Some claims suggest that the resin has the capability to completely eradiate infection, but those claims have not been supported by consistent findings. Mastic's antifungal, antibiotic, and antioxidant properties may all be contributors to its efficacy in inhibiting *H. pylori* proliferation, but the exact mechanism is not completely understood (Huwez 1998).

Mastic is typically dried and sold in capsule form. For *H. pylori*, a dosage of one to two grams per day for two weeks has been shown to be highly effective with 90 percent of patients being symptom free and 80 percent of patients showing negative stool-sample results (Dabos 2010).

Unfortunately, many people are unable to tolerate mastic in the quantities necessary to be effective in treating *H. pylori*. For some, mastic use results in side effects as bad as, if not worse than, the *H. pylori* symptoms they were originally experiencing.

It should be noted that there have been some clinical studies that have shown mastic to have no efficacy against *H. pylori* whatsoever.

Since the discovery of *H. pylori* in 1982, there has been a shift in the spectrum of gastrointestinal disorders. GERD and esophageal cancer have seen a substantial increase, while peptic ulcer and gastric cancer have seen a substantial decrease. This furthers the suggestion that *H. pylori* may have a protective effect against GERD and that, perhaps, alleviation of the bacteria is of more long-term benefit than full eradication.

Low Stomach Acid

Even once *H. pylori* levels are eliminated or brought under control, some people still suffer from stomach upset due to low stomach acid—either from PPI treatment or from the acid-lowering effects of the bacteria. Many doctors will have patients believe that stomach upset is often caused by acid levels being too high, but this isn't always the case. Once it is determined that low stomach acid levels might be of issue, measures should be taken to raise stomach acid levels back up into the normal range.

Symptoms of Low Stomach Acid Levels	
headaches	chronic fatigue
allergies	asthma
unexplainable aches and pains	osteoporosis
osteoarthritis	various cancers[3]

---

[3]   Wright, 2016.

Supplements Taken with Meals that Raise Stomach Acid Levels	
glutamine + pepsin + betaine lemon or lime water apple cider vinegar	bromelain sipping pineapple juice[4]

Symptoms of Ulcer		
abdominal pain or discomfort	lack of appetite	ulcers that bleed can cause a low blood count and fatigue
bloating	nausea or vomiting	weight loss
feeling full after eating a small amount of food	dark or tar-colored stools	burping[5]

Trials of Treatment

Choosing a suitable proton pump inhibitor is not easy. I tried Nexium first, only because, as a doctor, I had a ton of samples given to me by a sales representative. It didn't help at all with my reflux, and I experienced dizzy spells, which vanished once I stopped the medication.

Next I tried Protonix. It didn't work.

My husband likes Prevacid, so I decided to give that a try next. It seemed to help with my symptoms, but it still bothered me that I was treating symptoms, rather than getting to the root cause of my problem.

My treating physician tried to focus on eradicating *H. pylori*, prescribing the first regimen of medication. The first trial was to take omeprazole (Prilosec), 20 mg twice daily, plus amoxicillin, 1 g twice daily,

---

4   "The Importance of HCL," 2016.

5   Johnson, 2015.

plus clarithromycin (Biaxin), 500 mg twice daily. I failed the first treatment miserably. I didn't tolerate Prilosec well, so I didn't take it religiously. However, I knew how important it was to take a PPI because the bug likes an acidic environment.

My second trial regimen was with bismuth subsalicylate (Pepto-Bismol), 525 mg four times daily, plus metronidazole (Flagyl), 250 mg four times daily, plus tetracycline, 500 mg four times daily, plus a histamine H2 blocker. I could not tolerate Flagyl, as it caused a tingling sensation in my extremities that I simply could not deal with. Also, my father was on this antibiotic right before he passed away, and it brought with it painful memories.

My third trial regimen involved taking a different antibiotic for fourteen days. My physician has used amoxicillin, clarithromycin tetracycline, and I found out by a breath test that this had finally eradicated the bug.

Once my treatment was finished, my reflux improved, and I began to gain weight. Growing up in China, they always said that if you gain weight it means you have good nutrition and are generally healthier. I was happy, but I did still have frequent laryngitis with a sore throat. I use to have a beautiful voice; now I'm barely able to sing. I can hide the effects while singing in a large group, like a church, but I learned that what I had was reflux laryngitis, so obviously by eradicating *H. pylori*, I had only fixed one piece of the puzzle.

I tested my husband for *H. pylori*, and he was negative. I don't know where I originally got the bug, possibly from when I lived in a rural area when I was a teenager or from transmission from my mother, as most *H. pylori* infections occur in childhood. But before my mother died, I tested her, and she too was negative. Now that I had been treated, what still needed treating? I repeated a breathing test for *H. pylori*, and it was negative. But all my current symptoms were persistent; there was no resolution, no need to repeat the *H. pylori* treatment.

Now another differential diagnosis suggested the possibility that my previous infection had caused atrophic gastritis and that, for some reason, the symptoms had only recently become more advanced. I needed to learn more to decide if the atrophic gastritis from previous *H. pylori* caused me to have atrophic gastritis to cause the current symptoms.

Chapter 3

Endoscopy

I finally scheduled my endoscopy test.

With pressure from my family, I finally agreed to get an endoscopy done, to see what was going on once and for all. Making the decision to have an endoscopy was almost less difficult than making the appointment to have it done! My previous GI physician, who did an endoscopy for me in 1999, was New York University faculty. After Hurricane Sandy in 2012, his practice was compromised significantly. I called five times—both as a patient and then as a physician—and they never called me back.

Leave it to the younger generation to help in a different way. My daughter booked a consultation for me with this previous GI physician for the following week at 8:00 a.m. through ZocDoc's online doctor-booking services. This time their office called me back. They said the schedule was wrong, that Dr. G was unable to see me. So my daughter booked another NYU doctor at Conquer Medicine, again for the following week. Dr. S. is young (I tell myself I am old); he is also faculty at NYU. I decided to go forward with him. ZocDoc is an amazing resource, but you never want to just choose a doctor online; credentials are still important.

The following week I met the young Dr. S. I had written my own HIP (history of illness presentation). He listened attentively to everything I had to say about my condition and scheduled me for a 7:00 a.m. endoscopy— early so I could still get to work after the procedure.

I had had an endoscopy twelve years before, when I received my diagnosis of *H. pylori*. They tried to give me local lidocaine first, but it didn't work for me. The nurse then gave me Versed, a short-lasting benzodiazepine.

In the past decade, there has been a rapid advance in the types of medicines available. The standard endoscope is assisted by an anesthesiologist who administers Propofol, a short-lasting anesthesia, to assist the procedure. As a neurologist, I had no experience with the medication, but my husband mentioned to me that a Propofol overdose was what killed Michael Jackson. I would have to look up the side effects. I called Dr. S. to discuss my concerns, and he assured me I would be receiving a very small dose, so it should be of no concern.

On the day of the procedure, my husband and I left the house at 5:30 a.m. so I could arrive at the clinic by 6:30 a.m. We waited forty-five minutes before the nurse called us into the procedure room. The room was huge—maybe ten beds or more with full medical staff—nurses, GI doctors, anesthesiologist, medical assistants, everyone in scrubs.

They gave me an IV and then asked me some questions and to repeat my name. Very quickly I lost consciousness. It was amazing how quickly the medication took effect. Overall the procedure was very short with no discomfort. Twelve years earlier my throat was sore for at least a week post-procedure, and I'd had trouble swallowing. This time I woke up to Dr. S. standing over me, smiling and telling me that everything looked good—no cancer; I may just have had a small hiatal hernia.

I was very relieved! A nurse was required to take me to the elevator once I was ready to leave. I told the receptionist that I felt fine and did not require any assistance. The moment I started speaking, an unsteady wave hit me, but I was able to overcome it quickly. My husband was waiting for me downstairs. I ate breakfast and went on to see my 9:00 a.m. patients. I felt 100 percent normal.

While I was relieved to know I had no malignancy, I still had symptoms that needed to be addressed. At this point my physician had done all he could and would have no further suggestions. I knew I was completely on my own to figure out and resolve whatever conditions were continuing to cause these symptoms.

I felt like I had just found a new continent; all of my symptoms could be explained by a hiatal hernia. I rethought my diagnosis: my earlier infection with *H. pylori* caused a prolonged and recurrent bronchitis. I now had sensitive lungs. Maybe the severe coughing from the recurrent bronchitis had caused the hiatal herniation.

Chapter 4

Is Hiatal Hernia (HH) the Answer to My Symptoms?

When my dyspepsia symptoms continued, I began to wonder if I had some other condition contributing to my symptoms. It fascinates me to search for answers, and I came across hiatal hernia as a distinct possibility. From the preliminary findings of the endoscopy, I finally told myself I had a hiatal hernia.

In fact, when I spoke to my daughter, a third-year medical student at the time, about my symptoms, the first question she asked was, "What kind of hernia do you have?" If I did have a hiatal hernia, Dr. S. said it was very small. I had to wait to see the formal pathology report. Dr. S. had not given me my treatment options, and at this point, I was just glad the procedure went smoothly and there was no evidence of malignancy.

What Is Hiatal Hernia?

A hernia occurs when an internal organ presses into an area it isn't supposed to. Normally the stomach sits below the diaphragm. A hiatal hernia forms when the stomach pops up into the chest cavity through the hiatus, an opening in the diaphragm where the esophagus goes through in order to attach to the stomach. With a portion of the stomach above the diaphragm, it becomes more difficult for the lower esophageal sphincter to prevent acid from coming up into the esophagus. This is how a hiatal hernia can cause reflux (Delgado 2015).

Types of Hiatal Hernias

Sliding: The most common type of hiatal hernia, this is when the section of the stomach where esophagus and stomach join creeps up into the chest cavity through the hiatus (Delgado 2015).

Paraesophageal: The less-common type of hiatal hernia, it is more serious in nature. With a paraesophageal hiatal hernia, the esophagus stays in place, but a portion of the stomach pops through the hiatus and situates next to the esophagus. While it is possible to be asymptomatic with this type of hernia, there is a risk of the displaced portion of stomach becoming strangulated, cutting off its blood supply (Delgado 2015).

Normal Stomach Anatomy

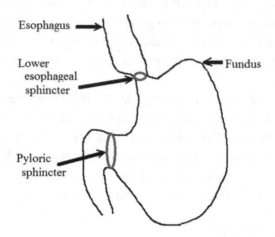

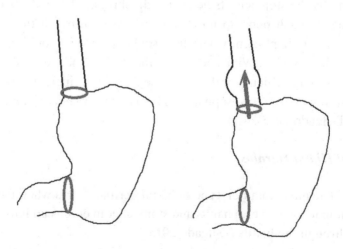

Normal stomach

Hiatal hernia

What Causes a Hiatal Hernia?

It is difficult, if not impossible, to pinpoint the exact cause of a hiatal hernia. Some people are born with larger hiatal openings and are therefore predisposed to developing hiatal hernias at some point in their lives.

Hiatal hernias typically occur in people over fifty but can occur at any age. According to the Esophageal Cancer Awareness Association, 60 percent of people will have a hiatal hernia by the time they are sixty years old.

Increased abdominal pressure plays a role in the development of hiatal hernia. Obesity, pregnancy, coughing, tight-fitting clothing, vomiting, poor posture, hard blows to the abdomen, heavy lifting, or straining during bowel movements can all be factors, but improper lifting is the most common mechanical cause of hiatal hernia. When lifting properly, all air must be expelled out of the lungs, otherwise the pressure of the lift could force the stomach up into the esophagus. Other traumas that could contribute include abdominal surgery, the impact of jumping from a significant height, horseback riding, strenuous abdominal exercise, doing a belly flop into a pool, impact from a fall, or the exertion from holding one's breath (Delgado 2015).

There are other causes of hiatal hernia.

Dietary: While it isn't completely clear which comes first, it is clear that a swollen ileocecal valve—the valve between the small and large intestines that limits contents of the colon from backing up into the ileum—is unable to close properly. People with hiatal hernia oftentimes have a swollen ileocecal valve. When this occurs, increased production of gas puts pressure on the stomach and causes it to press more tightly against the diaphragm, either causing hiatal hernia or exacerbating the problem (Horne 2010).

Emotional: You may have heard the sayings, "Swallow your anger" and "Can't stomach it." These sayings may have some physiological basis, and many natural practitioners believe that hiatal hernia can be caused by emotional stress and unexpressed anger (Horne 2010).

Another cause of hiatal hernia, as well as other health problems, that is gaining more attention from medical professionals and the media is sitting for prolonged periods, particularly with poor posture, such as slouching forward. Prolonged sitting is now being deemed the "silent killer," and with good reason. Studies under the umbrella term "inactivity studies" have shown that even regular aerobic activity won't counterbalance a lifestyle crafted around a desk or a sofa (or both). When sitting, electrical activity to your leg muscles slows to the point of almost stopping, beginning a cascade of harmful effects. Compared to walking around, your calorie-burning rate immediately drops by two-thirds. Within twenty-four hours of being sedentary, your insulin effectiveness drops, causing your risk of type-2 diabetes to rise. The enzymes responsible for breaking down fats in the bloodstream decrease in number, causing your HDL or good cholesterol to fall. In short, studies have estimated that with every hour you spend on the sofa, your risk of dying rises by 11 percent. Men who sit for an average of six hours per day have a death rate 20 percent higher than those who sit far less, while women who sit for six or more hours per day have a death rate 40 percent higher! Bottom line, excessive sitting does not preserve your energy; it saps you of it while shaving years off of your life (Vlahos 2011).

At this point, I was pretty certain I had a mild sliding hernia caused by my incessant coughing during my now-annual bronchitis. Taking cough medication is very important in preventing things like abdominal herniation and bleeding of the eye fundi.

Ever since September 11, 2001, I have suffered from bronchitis. I was there in Manhattan when the Twin Towers went down. The downtown hospital I have worked in since 1997 was thick with dust that day. It was visible in the air, on the desks, on the floor, everywhere. I couldn't be certain that my bronchitis was directly caused by that environmental pollution, but I did not wear a mask that day because I wasn't aware of the risks or dangers of breathing all of that in.

Symptoms of Hiatal Hernia
heartburn; regurgitation (GERD)
difficulty swallowing
chest pain radiating from below the breastbone
a bloated feeling after eating
shortness of breath
frequent belching
heart palpitations (due to irritation of the vagus nerve)[6]

The majority of patients who have hiatal hernias have no symptoms. Suggested treatment includes eating small amounts food frequently throughout the day (rather than just three meals a day), avoiding heavy foods or large quantities of food. I wanted to find out if all of my symptoms could be explained through a diagnosis of hiatal hernia—particularly the mystery symptom of a cold or hot sensation simultaneously in my stomach and abdomen right after I eat or even after the first couple of bites (Delgado 2015).

There are many fascinating aspects of the digestive system. One in particular is the vagus nerve. The vagus nerve extends from the brain to the abdomen and is responsible for such involuntary tasks as maintaining constant heart rate, autonomic regulation of the lungs, gastrointestinal peristalsis, sweating, keeping the larynx open for breathing, and controlling various muscle movements in the mouth responsible for speech (by way of the recurrent laryngeal nerve). The vagus affects every major organ with the exception of the adrenal glands.

The vagus is also responsible for certain functions of food processing, such as controlling the expansion of the stomach as food travels into it, helping break food into smaller particles through contractions of the stomach, the release of gastric acid, and helping to control sensations of hunger and fullness (Sircus 2014).

When people with a hiatal hernia eat, food may push up into the hernia bag, which in turn could touch the vagus nerve. This stimulation gives a signal to the stomach to secrete acid. In normal people, the secretion of acid is triggered mainly by a chemical reaction when food enters the mouth.

---

6   Delgado, 2015.

To better understand digestion, let's take a look at the process food undergoes once it enters our body.

The actual chemical process of digestion begins before food even enters the mouth. Taste, sight, and smell all stimulate the salivary glands to produce saliva in anticipation of food entering the mouth. Once food enters the mouth, nerves in the cheeks and tongue signal the brain to begin the process of secreting gastric juices.

Food is broken down through a process known as mastication, during which teeth break the food into smaller pieces while saliva softens the food and an enzyme in the saliva called amylase begins to break down carbohydrates into simple sugars. The tongue then rolls the softened pieces of food into small balls, or boluses, in preparation for swallowing.

The bolus moves to the throat, where rings of muscles push it into the esophagus, after which it makes its way into the stomach. Now that food has reached the stomach, it touches the lining, leading to the production of more gastric juices.

The gastric juices of the stomach are comprised of hydrochloric acid and pepsin, a protein-digesting enzyme. Pepsin breaks proteins into polypeptides and peptides, which stimulate the stomach lining to release gastrin (a hormone that, among other things, induces pancreatic secretions and emptying of the gallbladder) into the bloodstream. Gastrin circulates throughout the body, eventually reaching the stomach, where it signals the stomach lining to produce more gastric juices. The stomach then churns the food into chyme, a semiliquid paste that then passes into the small intestine.

The vagus nerve is responsible for peristalsis, the rhythmic contractions that move chyme through the small intestine toward the large intestine. The small intestine is where the continuation of the digestive process occurs alongside the absorption of nutrients from the food (Sircus 2014).

The small intestine is comprised of three sections: the duodenum, the jejunum, and the ileum. The duodenum connects with the lower portion of the stomach, where chyme is further broken down via enzymes and is introduced to pancreatic juices, intestinal juices, and bile. Pancreatic juices consist of three enzymes: amylase (the enzyme also found in saliva that breaks down carbohydrates), maltase (the enzyme that breaks maltose down into glucose), and lipase (an enzyme that breaks fats down into fatty acids). Bile, produced by the gallbladder, enters the duodenum and helps dissolve fats, which makes the fats more effectively broken down by lipase.

In the jejunum, the next segment of the small intestine, most of the nutrients from the broken-down food are absorbed before passing to the final segment, the ileum, where vitamin B12 is absorbed before passing the food remnants into the large intestine. There water is extracted from the products of digestion (which consist of undigested food, bacteria, and sloughed-off cells from the walls of the digestive tract) and circulated back into the bloodstream. Finally all remnants are passed out of the body as feces ("Digestive System" 2016).

But the vagus nerve, often termed "the wanderer" because it touches practically every major organ system in the body, when disrupted, could be the source of many conditions of ill health, extending beyond just digestive complaints. Some holistic-health practitioners postulate that up to 85 percent of the population may suffer from hiatal hernia syndrome. A hernia smaller than 2 cm may not be visible on barium films or endoscopy, so some people seeking answers for their health issues may walk away from diagnostics having been told that they do not have a hiatal hernia when, in fact, they have a very small herniation that is negatively impacting their health. The size of a hernia does not determine the health effects it may or may not cause. As stated above, many people with hiatal hernias remain asymptomatic or, at the very least, with an undetected condition (Sircus 2014).

As you can see, any disruption of the vagus nerve could wreak havoc on the digestive system as a whole. From swallowing to the churning of the stomach to peristalsis, which moves food through the digestive tract, all can be affected.

It makes sense that digestive dysfunction leads to constant imbalances throughout the body, but since the vagus nerve affects multiple body systems outside the digestive system, an irritation of this nerve can also cause disruptions of the heart, lungs, liver, gallbladder, pancreas, and colon. It is also linked to the kidneys, bladder, and external genitalia.

When a portion of the stomach is forced up into the hiatus, naturally the esophageal sphincter cannot function properly. This allows stomach contents to travel back up into the esophagus. The misplacement of the stomach can put pressure on the vagus nerve, which is partially responsible for signaling the secretion of stomach acid. This can lead to both overproduction and underproduction of hydrochloric acid and digestive enzymes.

Such misplacement can also affect the pyloric sphincter in such a way that digestive secretions enter the small intestine before they have completed their function, causing pH (acid-base) imbalance.

Low levels of hydrochloric acid, or hypochlorhydria, in the stomach will cause difficulty in digesting proteins and minerals by inhibiting the activation of pepsin, which functions only in an acidic environment. It may also cause food to putrefy in the intestines, causing a host of issues both short term and long term. Short term it may contribute to constipation; longer term it may contribute to food allergies, anemia, compromised immune function, as well as weakness of the glandular system. A low-acid environment in the stomach is linked with bacterial overgrowth, which makes a person more susceptible to food poisoning. Hypochlorhydria may lead to diarrhea and incomplete absorption of vitamins and nutrients, which may also lead to neuromuscular issues as well as other more serious conditions, including stomach cancer ("The Importance of HCL" 2016).

Symptoms of Low Stomach Acid
bloating, belching, and flatulence immediately after meals
heartburn, or GERD-like symptoms (often thought to be caused by *too much* stomach acid)
indigestion, diarrhea, or constipation
undigested food in stools.
stomach pains
acne
rectal itching
chronic candida[7]

A hiatal hernia may also disrupt the function of the diaphragm, the muscle that pulls down, allowing an expansion of the chest cavity so the lungs may inflate. Someone with a hiatal hernia may experience difficulty breathing or shallow breathing due to an inability to fully expand the chest cavity. Such a person may use his or her shoulders as a way of compensating by pulling the shoulders back to allow for more room.

---

[7] "The Importance of HCL," 2016.

In fact, one way to test for hiatal hernia is to place your fingers at the center of your abdomen just below the breastbone and take a deep breath. The area should expand upward and outward. If there area seems fixed, and you find yourself lifting your chest or adjusting your shoulders to breathe, it is possible you have a hiatal hernia (Horne 2009).

A sensation of a lump in the throat, difficulty swallowing, or food or capsules getting stuck may also be due to a hiatal hernia, which has caused a "kink" in the esophagus.

Conditions Associated with Hiatal Hernia	
Digestive	*Breathing and Circulation*
belching	difficulty with deep
bloating	abdominal breathing
heartburn	difficulty in swallowing
difficulty digesting meat/high-	capsules
protein foods	asthma
tension or pressure at the solar	inability to take a deep breath
plexus	from diaphragm
sensitivity at the waist	overall fatigue
intestinal gas	tendency to swallow air
regurgitation	allergies
hiccups	dry, tickling cough
lack or limitation of appetite	full feeling at base of throat
nausea, vomiting	pain or burning in upper chest
diarrhea	pressure in the chest
constipation	pain in the left side of the
colic in children	chest
difficulty in gaining weight or	pressure below breastbone
overweight	lung pain
ulcers	rapid heartbeat
	rapid rise in blood pressure
	pain in left shoulder, arm, or
	side of neck

Structural Issues	Other
TMJ (temporo-mandibular joint pain)	open ileocecal valve
bruxism (grinding teeth in sleep)	general weakness
	difficulty in getting and/or staying healthy
joint pain	overactive thyroid
localized or overall spinal pain	cravings for sugar or alcohol
headaches	*Candida albicans*
	menstrual or prostate problems
	urinary difficulties
	hoarseness
Stress	
suppression of anger or other emotions	
living with or having lived with a quick- tempered person	
dizziness	
shakiness	
mental confusion	
anxiety attacks	
insomnia	
hyperactivity in children[8]	

Treatment

A hiatal hernia is a mechanical problem and cannot be fixed with medication. Surgical procedures to correct hiatal hernia have mixed results because cutting into the area can weaken the structures surrounding it, increasing the chance of relapse. A good chiropractor or massage therapist with experience and understanding of the condition may be able to manipulate the stomach back into proper position by hand. This is the fastest and most effective mode of treatment.

It is possible to make self-adjustments, but they are not quite as effective (which isn't to say they don't work). Drink two full cups of warm

---

[8]   Horne, 2010.

water or tea and then rise up on your toes before dropping suddenly to your heels. Do this several times. The warm fluid should relax the stomach and diaphragm while providing weight in the stomach enough to allow gravity to pull down a mild hernia (Horne 2010).

The more I learned, the more convinced I became that I had a hiatal hernia, one that was small enough to go undetected by my endoscopy, and that this hernia was somehow irritating my vagus nerve. This "diagnosis" would explain my symptoms of heartburn, burning in the abdomen. This might also explain why my symptoms primarily occurred at dinner. During the day, the vagus nerve is much more tonic. Also, in the morning, the stomach is completely empty, too empty to cause food congestion, whereas at night, any undigested food from throughout the day could cause some sort of backup of undigested food or gastric juices.

My symptoms of heartburn diminished while taking probiotics and digestive enzymes, so I was not convinced that this was the only explanation for my symptoms. I began searching for natural ways to heal hiatal hernia.

Trail of the Treatment:

One way is to manipulate the stomach by using the right hand to press the left side at the base of the stomach, stroking firmly and suddenly, to push the herniation down (Horne 2010). Another is to drink several cups of warm water or tea, to relax the stomach and diaphragm, then jump from chair height to the ground, the idea being to use the force of gravity to pull the hernia down. This method concerned me, just because I worried about my knees, so I tried an easier alternative: drinking three cups of water before going for my morning jog. It seemed to help to some degree.

Another obvious part of the solution was to lose weight. I knew that at 142 pounds, I could easily stand to lose ten pounds.

During this time I also developed my five super soup. This soup has five major benefits:

- lowers blood pressure
- lowers blood sugar
- lowers cholesterol
- increases weight loss
- reduces cancer risk by increasing immune function

My prescription called for consuming three cups of soup for dinner, but typically I only had time for two. In the first month, I lost eight pounds. I continued my regimen. My symptoms improved even more, but they were still not completely gone.

Finally I received the reports of my endoscopy. I had no active gastritis, and there was no mention of hiatal herniation. I did have chronic gastritis with some atrophic gastritis at atrium. At this point I was in despair.

Chapter 5

Revisiting Atrophic Gastritis as the Possible Cause of My Symptoms

If there was no hiatal herniation, what was causing these symptoms?

After the final endoscopy findings, Dr. S. did not give any suggestions, assuming I would understand everything. I understood that my all symptoms were late effects of *H. pylori*. *H. pylorus* typically causes atrophic gastritis in the antrum, a portion of the pylorus near the bottom of the stomach, which separates the stomach from the duodenum (the first section of the small intestine). This was type-B atrophic gastritis that can decrease or impair the secretion of hydrochloric acid, pepsin, and intrinsic factor, leading to digestive problems. It also can cause stomach-mobility limitations (Hashimoto n.d.).

I reviewed my trials of treatment and responses to those trials. I was convinced that the majority of my symptoms were caused by a combination of atrophic gastritis and dysfunction of the LES.

Atrophic gastritis (AG) is a condition that can be caused by *H. pylori* infection or can be autoimmune in nature.

Autoimmune AG is caused by antibodies produced by your body attacking cells in your stomach that are responsible for secreting stomach acid and also a substance released by these cells called intrinsic factor that helps you absorb vitamin B12, a necessary nutrient in the production of red blood cells (Zayouna 2014).

There are two types of atrophic gastritis: type A, which tends to affect the corpus (body) or main portion of the stomach, and type B, which primarily affects the antrum or bottom portion of the stomach and which is most common in people with chronic *H. pylori* infection. Atrophic gastritis is a process that occurs when chronic inflammation of the stomach lining over a number of years leads to replacement of the gastric glandular cells by intestinal-type tissues. As a result, the stomach becomes impaired, unable to secrete the necessary amounts of hydrochloric acid, pepsin, and intrinsic factor (a glycoprotein that allows for the absorption of vitamin B12). This ultimately leads to digestive issues and nutritional deficiencies (Zayouna 2014).

Often there are no symptoms associated with AG, and therefore it can go unrecognized until associated symptoms of vitamin B12 deficiency and anemia appear. Most people diagnosed with AG are over fifty years of age (Zayouna 2014).

Symptoms of B12 Deficiency and Anemia
feelings of weakness lightheadedness dizziness chest pain paleness rapid pulse palpitations tinnitus (ringing in the ears)[9]

If you suspect you might be suffering from AG, your doctor will perform a physical examination, looking for tenderness over your stomach area or for any signs of B12 deficiency. Various blood tests will look for low levels of pepsinogen, high levels of gastrin, low B12 levels and antibodies against your own stomach cells and intrinsic factor. Further testing would include an endoscope to take stomach tissue samples to look for evidence of AG and/or the presence of *H. pylori*.

If you do have AG, treatment involves using antibiotic treatment in order to eradicate any *H. pylori* infection, along with PPI medication to reduce stomach acid, as *H. pylori* thrives in an acidic environment, and less acid will allow your stomach lining to heal more quickly.

If your AG is autoimmune rather than caused by *H. pylori*, you will receive B12 treatment.

It is not entirely clear as to whether eradication of *H. pylori* will stop or slow the progression of AG once it has begun. What is clear is that treatment will reduce your overall risk of stomach cancer.

---

[9]   Brunilda, 2015.

Risk Factors

The most common risk factor for developing atrophic gastritis is *H. pylori* infection. Since more than half of the world's population is infected with *H. pylori*, AG is very common (Zayouna 2014).

Autoimmune AG is very rare. People at greatest risk are those who suffer from thyroid disease or diabetes, African Americans or people of Northern European descent. People with either type of AG are at greater risk of developing stomach cancer (Zayouna 2014).

Prevention

There is no standard treatment for AG, but preventing the spread of *H. pylori* through the practice of good hygiene is key.

If I had AG, it was most definitely caused by *H. pylori* infection. I also knew my reactive hypergastrinemia put me in danger of developing ECL (enterochromaffin-like) cells, which are a type of cell that is found in the gastric glands of the gastric mucosa. Over a prolonged period of time, stimulation of these cells causes a proliferation of cell growth, which exacerbates hypergastrinemia and, in the case of gastrinoma (gastrin-secreting tumors in the pancreas and/or duodenum), can lead to complications such as the development of Zollinger-Ellison's syndrome (ZES). ZES stimulates the acid-producing cells in the stomach to maximum output, eventually causing ulceration of the stomach lining.

I had no idea that atrophic gastritis could result as an after-effect of HP infection, but there are also other factors that can lead to the breakdown of the mucosal lining in the stomach. Painkillers such as ibuprofen and aspirin, and excessive alcohol use are other causes.

Analysis of the Symptoms

I had mild fullness and congestion, along with a decreased appetite in 2009, after my mother passed away. A decreased appetite can result from grief. But it only happened at dinnertime. I thought maybe I was allergic to the freshly made bread I was eating at dinner. I looked at the ingredients of the bread, one of which was bleached flour. I switched brands to bread that did not have bleached flour and that also did not contain milk. With the switch, I had less fullness and congestion. I still had a sore throat on and off, also hoarseness, but I ignored both of those symptoms, as my overall condition seemed improved.

I continued to have recurrent bronchitis. I started taking an herbal remedy meant to boost the immune system, hoping to prevent further upper-respiratory infection. I took it at the first sign of sore throat. I would still get bronchitis once a year. I developed my own multivitamin, which ultimately helped reduce my instance of bronchitis.

My dyspepsia suddenly came back in force. I decided that my symptoms may have been caused by mild atrophic gastritis that caused my stomach to not produce enough acid to digest my food. My body was trying to compensate by secreting more hydrochloric acid (HCL). It was the lack of acid causing my feelings of indigestion, fullness, and frequent belching. But why did I have significant symptoms at dinnertime?

I checked into the secretion of digestive enzymes and gastric secretion cycles, which did not tell me why I was only experiencing symptoms in the evening. Bolstering my digestion was my next step in treating my symptoms. I needed to try something new.

I decided to try a treatment of helping digestion from a lack of acid secretion from atrophic gastritis.

Chapter 6

To Help Digestion, Is My Solution Trying Probiotics?

Early on in my quest for a natural cure for my digestive symptoms, I decided to try probiotics or "friendly" bacteria. As mentioned in the previous chapter on *H. pylori*, probiotics are "gut-friendly" bacteria or microbes that have a positive impact on digestion. Improved digestion, in turn, improves overall health. The most commonly studied probiotics are those that produce lactic acid, particularly *Lactobacillus acidophilus* and bifidus.

Probiotics are naturally found in fermented foods and drinks such as yogurt, sauerkraut, kombucha, raw pickles, miso, tempeh, and kimchi (to name a few). Cultures that typically consume fermented foods naturally get probiotics from their diet rather than through supplementation. Our Western culture typically eats a diet full of processed foods, devoid of healthful living organisms. This, coupled with a proliferation in antibiotic use (both for medical use and in the food system), has led to a microbially challenged populace.

We each share our body with somewhere around 100 trillion bacteria. They live on our skin, in our mouths, and in our intestines. In fact, one to two pounds of bacteria are found in our digestive tract alone. For every one cell that *is* us, that is to say makes up our intrinsic selves, there are somewhere around ten microbes that *inhabit* us.

Researchers have found that the microbes that inhabit us truly comprise a second genome and that damage to or disruption of that second genome can result in a plethora of health-related ill effects. On the flip side, a strong, balanced microbial population can lead to amazing health benefits (Gorbach 1996).

Fecal transplants, where the gut flora from a healthy individual are transplanted into the intestine of a compromised individual, have been used to effectively treat *C. difficile*, a serious antibiotic-resistant bacteria that typically affects people who have previously had antibiotic treatment for other infections. When a person takes antibiotics, good bacteria are typically wiped out along with the bad. Without a substantial replenishment of friendly microbes, pathogenic microbes have a chance to take root and wreak havoc on their hapless host. When a healthy population of friendly microbes is present in the intestinal tract, they provide ample competition for pathogenic microbes, keeping their unfriendly populace at bay (Fecal transplantation is performed 2016). This is one reason why one person might eat a meal and get food poisoning, while another person may eat the same food and have no ill effects whatsoever.

Researchers have found that transplanting the flora from lean mice into mice with compromised metabolic systems improved the compromised mice's sensitivity to insulin, improving their overall metabolic health. Other research points to compromised gut flora and an increase in food sensitivities and allergies (Festi 2014).

Our relationship with our gut flora extends beyond the digestive tract, as these microbes help in the manufacture of short-chain fatty acids, amino acids, neurotransmitters (such as serotonin), enzymes, as well as vitamins B and K. All of these substances play roles in multiple systems throughout the body, indicating that what populates us may become a big component of who we are, even to a certain extent altering our mood or behavioral tendencies. When the gut microbes of relaxed, adventuresome mice are transplanted into mice that are generally timid and anxious, the once-timid and anxious mice become a bit more adventuresome (den Besten 2013). This makes an excellent case for keeping gut flora in healthy balance because if a healthy population of good microbes can have a positive outcome on behavior, it makes just as much sense that a proliferation of not-so-friendly microbes could have a negative effect on perhaps not only your behavior but your overall outlook on life.

As our microbes become us, our immune systems have a job to do. They need to learn, as our flora changes, which bacteria to recognize as "us" or friendly and which ones to consider invaders of the castle.

You may have heard the saying, "think with your gut." Well, as it turns out, there is so much more to that saying than we ever imagined. Our gut flora are highly adaptive and regenerative (sometimes turning over every twenty minutes) and are able to quickly make decisions whether to fight or eat a new substance that enters the digestive tract. It is this adaptive ability that allows our gut flora to evolve and respond, so we don't have to (Alcock 2014). By analogy, you don't need to know how to engineer a bridge in order to get across it.

The first product I turned to was a probiotic formula that was primarily (four out of the eight strains) comprised of *Lactobacillus* (see below), one bacterium commonly found in fermented foods such as yogurt and sauerkraut. *Lactobacillus* converts lactose and other sugars into lactic acid and is responsible for giving yogurt and sourdough bread their tangy taste. *Lactobacillus* has been studied for its anticancer and anti-inflammatory properties. It also helps to lower cholesterol by reducing cholesterol esters associated with saturated fatty acids in the blood. *Lactobacillus* breaks down bile salts, which reduces cholesterol absorption in the intestines (Lactobacillus 2016).

After taking this probiotic for the first time after a meal (even though the directions suggest taking it before), my stomach was comfortable and soothed. I felt amazing, like the sun had come out after a long and turbulent storm. My heartburn disappeared, and after two weeks of treatment, I no longer needed antacid medication on the weekends.

After three weeks of treatment, I was able to start eating foods I had been avoiding, like chocolate and dumplings. I understand the role of probiotics in digestion, but what I didn't understand was how they helped me, so I decided I needed to learn more.

Lactic acid-producing bacteria release acids, hydrogen peroxide, and substances toxic to other bacteria. The production of these substances helps to inhibit the growth of pathogenic organisms. But not all probiotics contain lactic acid-producing bacteria, nor are all probiotics created equal (Gorbach 1996).

The label of the product I was using claimed that each capsule contained five billion culture cells. That seems like a lot until you consider that is the number they guarantee at the time of packaging. Over time, the cultures die. Consider shipping time and time on the shelf in the store, and you are dealing with considerably fewer culture cells than are reflected in the claim on the box. There is no way of knowing, box to box, how many live culture cells you are actually consuming. Also consider that when you get your probiotics from fermented foods such as yogurt, sauerkraut, or kefir, the active live culture cells are in the trillions, not the billions.

Some people with GERD suffer from small-intestine bacterial overgrowth, which typically consists of an overgrowth of lactic acid-producing bacteria

(Chey 2010). Obviously, consuming lactic acid-producing bacteria will likely exacerbate rather than help people with this condition.

Aside from *Lactobacillus* and bifidobacteria, there are other probiotic organisms called soil-based organisms (SBO), which consist of bacteria that are, as the name suggests, found in soil. We naturally get these organisms on our hands when we do yard work or pot a houseplant. We get them from our vegetables if we haven't completely disinfected them prior to eating. In fact, SBOs were a normal part of our intestinal flora back before we decided we needed to live in sterile environments. Think of babies crawling around on the ground; this form of travel is also a form of inoculation. Today with hand sanitizer and produce disinfectant, we are getting fewer and fewer SBOs in our bodies. SBOs, unlike other strains of bacteria, are transient and need to be replenished as they are eventually flushed out of the digestive system. Supplementation with SBOs is controversial, as SBOs have the potential of becoming pathogenic if not kept in check. If a person has an already inadequately populated digestive tract, SBOs could potentially do more harm than good, although some people have reported that SBOs have helped cure them of a multitude of digestive issues. As always, it is best to check with your healthcare provider to see if this form of treatment might be right for you (Reinagel 2014).

Lactobacillus

Lactobacillus, a bacterium found in the urinary, genital, and digestive systems, has over fifty different species, most of which help with polysaccharide and protein digestion, as well as generating vitamins and short-chain fatty acids (Chey 2010).

Species	Health Benefits
Lactobacillus GG	Shown to reduce abdominal pain in children with IBS. Shown to reduce antibiotic-related diarrhea in children. Children taking *Lactobacillus GG* develop fewer lung infections while attending daycare. Shown to reduce the risk of traveler's diarrhea in adults.
Lactobacillus casei, Lactobacillus bulgaricus, Streptococcus thermophiles	Shown to decrease risk of antibiotic-related diarrhea in hospitalized adults.
Lactobacillus gasseri and Lactobacillus rhamnosus	Shown to lengthen time between bacterial vaginosis infections.[10]

Some of the other lactobacilli found in foods and supplements are *Lactobacillus acidophilus, L. acidophilus DDS-1, Lactobacillus plantarium, Lactobacillus reuteri, Lactobacillus salivarius,* and *Lactobacillus johnsonii,* most of which have health benefits linked to them such as preventing yeast infections, helping ease IBS (irritable bowel syndrome) symptoms, preventing UTIs, treating lactose intolerance, and helping relieve skin disorders such as eczema and acne. More studies need to be conducted before any such benefits can be claimed to be definitive (Lactobacillus 2016).

Bifidobacteria

There are approximately thirty species of bifidobacteria. They make up approximately 90 percent of the healthy bacteria in the colon. They appear in the intestinal tract within days of birth, especially in breastfed infants ("Bifidobacteria" 2016).

---

[10] "Lactobacillus," 2016.

Species	Health Benefits
Bifidobacterium infantis	When given to patients with irritable bowel syndrome, patients showed improvement of symptoms.
Bifidobacterium lactis	Shown to lower LDL cholesterol in people with type-2 diabetes. Shown to raise HDL cholesterol in adult women. Shown to improve glucose tolerance in pregnant women.[11]

Some other strains of bifidobacteria that are used as probiotics are *Bifidobacterium bifidum, Bifidobacterium longum, Bifidobacterium breve, Bifidobacterium thermophilum*, and *Bifidobacterium pseudolongum*. Some Bifidobacteri-a may offer health benefits such as inhibiting the growth of harmful bacteria in the intestines and regulating immune responses, repressing cancer-causing enzymatic activity within a host's "microbiome," (the human microbiota consists of the ten to one hundred trillion symbiotic microbial cells harbored by each person, primarily bacteria in the gut; the human microbime consists of the genes these cells harbor), producing vitamins, and conversion of certain dietary compounds into readily absorbable nutrients ("Bifidobacteria" 2016).

Saccharomyces boulardii

The only yeast probiotic, *S. boulardii* has been shown to help alleviate diarrhea associated with antibiotic use and traveler's diarrhea ("Saccharomyces boulardii" 2016).

Streptococcus thermophilus

This probiotic produces high levels of lactase, which may help some people with lactose intolerance ("Bifidobacteria" 2016).

---

[11]   "Bifidobacteria," 2016

The microbes in our gut fulfill many functions that go far beyond just aiding digestion. These microbes can also stimulate cell growth, can prevent proliferation of microorganisms that may by harmful while training the immune system to respond only to those harmful microorganisms, and also can prevent certain diseases.

Certain gut flora produce enzymes that we, as humans, lack for breaking down certain starches, fibers, lactose, sugar alcohols, and proteins. Without an adequate balance of intestinal microflora, a person may experience excess flatulence when consuming some or all of these substances (Alcock 2014).

Bacteria in the intestine help to ferment carbohydrates (sugars and various fibers) and then turn them into short-chain fatty acids (SCFAs) through a process called saccharolytic fermentation, which is the metabolization of sugar resulting in energy. This process also aids in the absorption of ions such as calcium, magnesium, and iron, as well as with the synthesis of vitamins like biotin and folate.

Other products of saccarolytic (natural sugars–based) fermentation include lactic acid; acetic acid (used by muscle; it is the main component if common vinegar); propionate, which helps the liver produce adenosine triphosphate (ATP), which transports chemical energy within cells for metabolism; and butyric acid, which is currently being studied for its anticancer and anti-inflammatory properties. Butyric acid (a component of vomit that gives it its distinctive smell) inhibits the growth of tumor cells in the colon while encouraging the growth of healthy epithelial cells. This phenomenon is not completely understood but is known as the "butyrate paradox." Butyrate encourages the production of regulatory T cells in the digestive tract. Patients suffering from inflammatory bowel disease typically lack butyric acid-producing gut microbes, therefore making the person deficient in butyrate. New research has shown significant improvement in mice suffering from colitis when treated with butyrate. Curiously, butyric acid is a component of human and mammalian body odor (Miller 1979).

A different type of fermentation, proteolytic fermentation, breaks down proteins in the digestive tract such as dead cells, collagen, and elastin found in food and enzymes. While this type of fermentation produces SCFAs, it also produces toxins and carcinogens, thereby pointing to the hazards of a diet that contains excessive amounts of protein (Ali 1998).

Fermentation, through the production of lactic acid and fatty acids, lowers the pH in the colon, which helps to discourage the proliferation of harmful bacterial species.

But how does your immune system know which "bugs" are helpful and which ones might cause you harm?

The bugs in your gut help with the expression of toll-like receptors (TLRs). TLRs act in much the same way as the National Guard might after a hurricane—assessing and then helping repair damage after an invasion or natural disaster.

TLRs, in conjunction with other pattern-recognition receptors (PRRs), give our gut the ability to discriminate between helpful and harmful bacteria by recognizing molecular patterns in pathogens that are not shared by host cells.

The ability of our gut flora to protect us from the invasion of pathogenic bacteria is only one of the ways in which these bugs help keep us "chugging along." Our intestinal "soldiers" also play a role in metabolizing the carcinogens present in our diet. Much focus has been given to the carcinogenic effect of cooking muscle meats at high temperatures, which produces heterocyclic amines (HCAs). HCAs can induce breast, prostate, pancreatic, and colon tumor formation. The National Cancer Institute's Division of Cancer Epidemiology and Genetics found that people who eat beef that is cooked medium well or well done are three times as likely to develop stomach cancer as those who eat beef that is prepared rare or medium rare (Cross 2007). The same does not hold true for items such as liver, dairy, or tofu.

In-vitro studies (meaning study outside of the biologic body) have shown that our gut flora can bind to mutagenic compounds found in meat cooked at high temperatures, indicating that a well-populated intestinal tract may provide an important line of defense against certain types of cancer (Cross 2007).

Intestinal flora have also been suggested to play a role in preventing allergies. Allergies develop when your immune system overreacts to substances that are otherwise not harmful. The gut flora of babies and small children with allergies differs from that of babies and children with allergies, in that the allergic children tend to have a higher instance of *C. difficile* and *S. aureus* and lower quantities of Bacteroides and Bifidobacteria. It is possible that since "good" bacteria train the immune system to differentiate between harmful and nonharmful antigens, a lack of good bacteria early on in life could lead to a poorly trained immune system ("Bifidobacteria" 2016).

While taking probiotics, my symptoms were almost gone. I still didn't completely understand the way probiotics helped my digestion with their subsequent antacid function, but what I did know was that a healthy balance of good microbes aided in acid digestion. As mentioned in the chapters on *H. pylori* and hiatal hernia, low stomach acid can cause symptoms most people would associate with high levels of stomach acid. Use of antacid medications can lower perhaps already low stomach acid levels, allowing opportunistic overgrowth of unfriendly microbes. Small-intestine bacterial overgrowth (SIBO) can cause symptoms that mimic irritable bowel syndrome, such as flatulence, abdominal bloating and distension, abdominal pain, diarrhea, and constipation. Mistaking low-stomach-acid dyspepsia for stomach acid excess and treating it with antacid medication can exacerbate the ills of an already unbalanced digestive system. Whatever the function of probiotics, they were working for me. After two weeks, my heartburn was completely gone.

Unfortunately, right around week three of taking probiotics, something went off track. I became androgenic, wired, and couldn't shut my mind or body down. My blood pressure became elevated, and I developed dysuria, or painful urination, along with an increased urge to urinate. I read an article stating that *Lactobacilli*, which is major bacterium of probiotics, can cause UTI (urinary tract infection) (Darbo 2008).

While the development of UTI, dysuria, and insomnia while on probiotics is very rare, common sense tells you that if you have introduced a new supplement to your routine and your health deteriorates, you should stop taking that supplement. I suspected that I had a bacterial overgrowth from taking a relative large quantity of the probiotics, so I only took one tab of Cipro antibiotic, and within one day, my symptoms disappeared. I was able to sleep, and my blood pressure went down. My husband and daughter couldn't believe my results, so I reintroduced the probiotic, and my symptoms returned right away. Four more days on the antibiotic, and all symptoms ceased. Typically a UTI caused by *E. coli* presents with chills and fatigue in conjunction with dysuria and urinary urgency and frequency. This was completely different.

I believe my body was fighting the friendly bacteria with adrenaline. It isn't completely unheard of for probiotics to have a negative effect on some people. Typically those people are immune-compromised individuals who were given probiotics as treatment for an underlying condition. In these cases, the probiotics stimulated the overgrowth of pathogenic bacteria and resulted in sepsis, but these cases are rare, particularly in otherwise healthy individuals.

I was learning that while all of the natural remedies I was trying helped, they too were not without side effects. There was, both literally and figuratively, no magic pill for my condition.

I began watching my diet. I started eating a vegetable soup every day. My symptoms were on again/off again, but overall I was making progress.

I was glad to be off of prescription medication and glad that, at this point, I was able to finally eat most of the food that I liked. I just had to be careful. For instance, if I ate an apple turnover (which has lots of butter), I felt discomfort. If I overate blueberries, all of my symptoms would quickly return. I reduced the dose of probiotics, taking one probiotic capsule in the morning for another month. I had no UTI but got benefit for my digestive symptoms, as probiotics helped my indigestion.

Chapter 7

Final Help of Digestive Enzymes

I finally figured out that my heartburn was not because of overflowing acid; it was because of indigestion. I knew I needed to help my digestion, as I did not have enough stomach acid and pepsin. I tried several kinds of digestive enzymes on the market. I finally decided on MRM Digest All. If I took one capsule after dinner, I was symptom free. My reflux disappeared. I finally found a way to heal my symptoms. Retrospectively, one of the facts of GERD is indigestion. Few doctors and almost no patients have approached their symptoms with help to digest rather than with PPI or antacid treatment.

I also tried some lemon water after meals; it also helped, as lemon helps digestion.

Enzymes are, in biological terms, catalysts. They are amino acids (proteins) secreted by your body that help physiological reactions occur faster than they otherwise would without them. They lower the amount of energy required by the body for certain reactions to occur. Some digestive actions would not be possible without enzymatic assistance ("Enzyme" 2016).

But enzymes are not just for digestion. Enzymes aid in all of your physiological processes. Scientists have identified more than three thousand different enzymes, but they believe there are thousands more waiting to be discovered.

Basic Enzyme Functions	
dissolving blood clots	oxygen absorption
distributing nutrients	reducing inflammation
energy production	regulating cholesterol and triglycerides
fighting infection	removing toxic waste
healing wounds	slowing down the aging process[12]
hormone regulation	

---

[12] "Enzyme," 2016.

For our discussion here, there are three types of enzymes: digestive, metabolic, and food-based.

Digestive Enzymes

Digestive enzymes, as the name implies, help you break food down into smaller parts so that the nutrients can be absorbed and transported throughout your body. These enzymes are produced by your pancreas and exist outside of your cells and even carry out other functions when food is not present in your system (which will be covered below).

Metabolic enzymes are enzymes that occur inside of your cells or are "intracellular." These enzymes help with specific cell functions.

Food-based enzymes, as the name suggests, are enzymes that you get from your food—particularly raw food—that help you with the digestive process. The more enzymes you get from your food, the less taxed your body is to produce enzymes to help you with the digestive process, leaving your own enzymes to help with extradigestive functions.

The Western diet typically is comprised of more than 50 percent ultraprocessed food (Steele 2016). This includes "whole-grain" pastas, flours, and breads; natural sugar substitutes; cereals; juices; even milk. Yes, milk (unless you are consuming raw milk) is a processed food that has been heavily pasteurized, denaturing proteins and killing valuable enzymes.

Diets that contain cooked, processed foods, along with overuse of antibiotics, can contribute to enzyme deficiency. Cooking foods at oven temperatures above 116° F causes enzymes to become denatured by changing their fragile structure, therefore making them unusable to our bodies (Pope 2016). This is one reason why eating a raw diet can be beneficial, as it allows naturally occurring enzymes in the food to remain intact, decreasing taxation of the body to produce its own enzymes that can then be used instead for supporting the immune system and overall healing of the gut. This is how chronic deficiency can lead to disease—when your enzymes are depleted, you may not have proper healing capabilities, proper immune support, or proper physiological function.

There are three stages of digestion: mechanical (which takes place when food is broken down in the mouth by chewing and by enzymes in the saliva), chemical (when food is churned and mixed with hydrochloric acid and pepsin in the stomach), and enzymatic (when enzymes work on breaking down the products of digestion to a point where they can be absorbed through the walls of the small intestine). The last stage is where nutrients are absorbed into the bloodstream. If this process isn't functioning optimally, a host of issues will arise.

I decided to try digestive enzymes as part of my treatment. The first one I tried only contained one type of enzyme, and it did not work for me. The second one I tried was more of a broad-spectrum product. It contained twelve different enzymes along with an herbal blend that lends itself to better digestion.

The bottle said to take two capsules before each meal. With one capsule, most of my symptoms disappeared! There was no full, congested feeling, no stomach burning, almost no reflux. I also began to enjoy better-quality sleep. Typically I would experience insomnia at least once a week, but on the enzymes, that disappeared. I was amazed.

I asked my husband to try taking the enzymes, and they also helped him. Later I introduced them to all my family members. One of my sisters had told me that she couldn't have dinner later than a certain time or she experienced severe indigestion that kept her up all night, so I gave some to her as well.

Obviously, if I experienced such quick relief by taking these enzymes, it meant that my body was not producing enough enzymes on its own. Since enzymes helped to break down the food for proper digestion, perhaps my body was secreting more acid to help make up for the lacking enzymes.

The more I learned, the more the puzzle pieces began to come together. Antibiotic treatment can inhibit enzyme production by decreasing the population of intestinal flora, and intestinal flora produce enzymes that make certain nutrients, such as vitamin K, biotin, B12, folic acid, and thiamine and various minerals more absorbable to the body (Hill 1997). Antibiotics also function as enzyme inhibitors by working on the exterior of the bacterial cell, causing weakness, which eventually causes the bacteria to burst.

The enzymes produced by our gut flora also play a role in something called enterohepatic circulation, a process by which biliary acids, bilirubin, estrogens, cholesterol, drugs, and metabolites of vitamin D are metabolized in the liver, excreted in bile, and then passed into the intestine, where they are reabsorbed through the intestinal mucosa and returned once again to the liver. Enterohepatic circulation involves substances that are joined together in the liver. Enzymes produced by intestinal flora help to break the bonds between these substances, in order to make them more easily absorbable through the intestinal wall. Antibiotics inhibit enterohepatic circulation by diminishing the population of intestinal flora, thereby decreasing the production of these enzymes ("Enterohepatic Circulation" 2016).

You can imagine the effect. If someone has been given antibiotic treatment and they are also taking another type of drug that undergoes enterohepatic circulation, such as birth-control pills, where estrogen is vital to efficacy, the blood-plasma level of the drug and the half-life of the drug will be diminished.

I thought back to my yearly bronchitis and the fact that taking antibiotics to treat this condition likely played a role in gradually diminishing my intestinal flora and thereby part of my enzyme-producing capabilities. I also knew that over time, as we age, our bodies tend to produce fewer enzymes. This, in conjunction with eating a Western diet of highly cooked and processed foods, can lead to issues stemming from enzyme deficiency. I decided to try enzyme therapy as part of my treatment for my GI symptoms.

I began to ask some of my patients and community members who suffered from acid reflux and heartburn symptoms to rethink their treatment plans. While the fruits of the pharmaceutical industry have their place (proton pump inhibitors, H2 blockers, antacids), I wanted everyone to stop just treating their symptoms and to really get to the root of what was causing them.

Ninety percent of nutrient absorption occurs in the small intestine, where most digestive enzymatic function takes place (Barron 2016). This is where nutrients are absorbed into your bloodstream through the villi in the intestinal wall. Imagine if this process was not functioning optimally or at all.

Enzyme production begins to decline starting at age twenty and continues to decline at a steady rate of approximately 13 percent every ten years (Mercola 2011). This could explain why people are not able to eat and drink like they used to or, over time, lost a taste for what used to be their favorite foods or beverages.

To complicate things further, as you age you produce less hydrochloric acid, which plays a crucial role in activating many of your digestive enzymes.

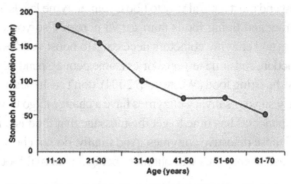

Fig. 1. Contrary to popular belief, stomach acid secretion tends to decline with advancing age. This graphs shows mean stomach acid secretion from the second decade to the eighth decade. (From *"Why Stomach Acid is Good For You."*)

Metabolic Enzymes

Scientists have a hard time agreeing how many cells you have in your body, but estimates range anywhere from 37.2 trillion to 100 trillion. No matter what the number, every last one of your cells relies on metabolic enzymes to catalyze energy production in order to grow, reproduce, repair tissue, and respond to your environment ("Three Enzyme Categories" 2016).

Some Systems Affected by Metabolic Enzymes	
bone maintenance	lymphatic function
cardiac function	muscle maintenance
circulatory function	neurological function
endocrine function	renal function (kidney)
hepatic function (liver)	reproductive function
joint maintenance	skin maintenance

Food-Based Enzymes

Food-based enzymes, as the name implies, are enzymes derived from the consumption of living foods, those rich in bacteria and enzymes that aid in the digestion of those foods. Once you heat foods above a certain temperature (the arguable range is anywhere from 104° to 118° F), bacteria begin to die off, and enzymes become denatured and unusable by the body ("Three Enzyme Categories" 2016).

The easiest and most natural way to boost your enzyme levels is to consume a diet rich in raw and living foods (aim for 75 percent), so you can get all of the amino acids and enzyme cofactors necessary to boost your own metabolic enzyme production, consume fewer calories (some people spend 10 to 15 percent of their energy digesting food (Westerterp 2004), don't rush meals—chew your food completely so your salivary enzymes have a chance to go to work on your food and your pancreas has time to get the message that food is on its way and to "crank out" those digestive enzymes. And finally, do not chew gum, as this causes the release of enzymes without there being any actual food to digest.

Enzyme-Rich Foods	
avocado	mango
bee pollen	papaya
extra virgin olive oil	pineapple
extra coconut olive oil	raw dairy
grapes	raw honey
kiwi	raw meat

Symptoms of Possible Enzyme Deficiency		
acne	fatigue	irritable bowel syndrome
allergies	hair loss	joint pain
arthritis	hair thinning	mood swings
bloating	hay fever	neck and shoulder aches
chronic fatigue	headaches	PMS
cold hands and feet	heart problems	psoriasis
chronic common colds	hot flashes	rashes
constipation	hypoglycemia	sinus infections
depression	immune suppression	sprue (celiac disease)
diarrhea	indigestion	weak nails
diverticulitis	inflammation	weight gain[13]
dull skin	insomnia	

---

[13] James, 2016.

Once I incorporated broad-spectrum digestive enzymes into my routine, I found that I felt more nutritionally balanced. My insomnia improved, and my temper improved (even under stress). I just felt better.

I stopped taking a vitamin supplement that I had developed because I realized that taking in the proper nutrition—whether through balanced diet or through diet and supplementation—doesn't matter if your body is unable to metabolize those nutrients.

Suddenly I was able to eat tomatoes and slightly heavy food. I deviated from the suggested usage by taking a capsule after my meal rather than before because I wanted my own enzymes to start working first.

Over time I had less and less of sore throat from reflux laryngitis after eating. For years I had awakened feeling congested. I always thought I was allergic to the sheets, the laundry detergent, the down in our comforter, or dust from the nightstand. Once I started taking the enzymes, my congestion disappeared.

My immune system also grew stronger. The first winter after starting on enzymes, I did get my yearly bronchitis, but it was much milder, and I did not require antibiotic treatment, as I recovered in just two weeks.

Prior to taking enzymes, my B12 levels were low, which is common in people who have atrophic gastritis. The body tends to store anywhere from a three- to five-year supply of B12 in the liver, but with atrophic gastritis, the mucosal lining of the stomach is replaced with fibrous tissue ("Vitamin B12" 2016). This inhibits the secretion of stomach acid, pepsin, and something called intrinsic factor, which is necessary for absorption of vitamin B12. Over time the body depletes its stores and, without supplementation, AG sufferers may become deficient.

Once I began taking enzymes, my B12 levels returned to normal, without supplementation. This proved to me that my body had simply not been producing enough enzymes on its own to properly help make the nutrients in my food bioavailable.

The enzyme haptocorrin (R-factor) is released by the salivary glands and binds to B12 in the stomach, where it protects the vitamin from hydrochloric acid. Once it reaches the duodenum, the B12 and haptocorrin are disjoined, and the B12 binds to intrinsic factor (IF), a glycoprotein produced by the parietal cells in the stomach. Once the B12 and intrinsic factor have joined, it is finally able to be absorbed by the small intestine (Jensen 2011).

It would seem that in my case, I had enough R-factor and IF, but one piece of the puzzle to the body's ability or inability to absorb B12 has to do with a different enzyme, protease, which is responsible for breaking down proteins, in this case the binding proteins of haptocorrin and intrinsic factor. Without protease, the binding proteins would remain joined to B12 and would not be able to be absorbed in the small intestine.

It is very common for people's digestive abilities to decrease with age. It is likely that the quantity and perhaps quality of the enzymes produced will diminish over time. People will notice that they are unable to eat the same type or quantity of food they once were. This, of course, can be caused by other factors—decrease in physical activity being one of them—but people generally don't talk to their doctors unless they are suffering a prolonged physical symptom such as heartburn. Typically a doctor will recommend eating smaller meals and might prescribe an acid-lowering medication. Very rarely is indigestion considered as part of the differential diagnosis for heartburn. When a patient presents with chronic heartburn, a doctor might call for an endoscopy, which might produce inconclusive results because the symptoms the patient is experiencing are not necessarily caused by a lesion (although that can result if the problem is left unchecked), but is rather a systemic functional deficit or dysfunction.

The more I have researched my own condition, the more my thinking as a doctor has changed. I realize that treating symptoms is not enough. Finding the true root cause of a condition is the only way to not only fully treat that condition but to teach prevention as well.

The more I looked into the role of various enzymes, the more I realized that this could have been a major missing piece to my puzzle all along.

If you were to consult WebMD concerning potential causes of indigestion, they would give you the following list of possible factors:

Diseases:	Medications:
ulcers GERD stomach cancer (rare) gastroparesis (a condition where the stomach doesn't empty properly; this often occurs in diabetics) stomach infections irritable bowel syndrome chronic pancreatitis thyroid disease	aspirin and many other painkillers estrogen and oral contraceptives steroid medications certain antibiotics thyroid medicines Lifestyle: eating too much, eating too fast, eating high-fat foods, or eating during stressful situations drinking too much alcohol cigarette smoking stress and fatigue[14]

While WebMD does mention that *sometimes* people have indigestion unrelated to these factors, called functional or nonulcer dyspepsia, they do not mention anything about enzyme deficiency or potential issues stemming from antibiotic treatment.

As with any system in the body, if you are deficient in one area, it can throw the entire system off balance. For instance, up to 40 percent of people who are deficient in pancreatic enzymes suffer, likely without knowing, with bacterial overgrowth in their small intestine (Bures 2010). They may walk around feeling bloated, crampy, and sluggish; they may have heartburn or be oversensitive to pain (fibromyalgia).

In addition to an overgrowth that could cause fibromyalgia-like symptoms, enzyme deficiencies can mimic any number of conditions that might cause a doctor to reach for his or her prescription pad. For instance, an inability to properly digest fats could result in symptoms very similar to a malfunctioning gallbladder.

---

[14]   "Indigestion," 2016.

But what causes enzyme deficiencies? As mentioned above, we tend to produce fewer enzymes as we age. Also, unlike a diet rich in raw and fermented foods, a Western diet is chock full of overcooked and highly processed foods that are devoid of any naturally occurring enzymes. Emotional and environmental stressors also inhibit the body's ability to produce enzymes.

Our diets are comprised of five basic nutrient groups: fat, protein, sugars, carbohydrates, and fiber. Without the necessary enzymes to break these components down, we may become intolerant to a particular food. For example, some people are thought to become vegetarians not for social, environmental, or political reasons, but because their body does not produce enough protease to break down the proteins in meat. This might cause them to conclude (consciously or subconsciously) that meat does not agree with them, leading them to eat a meat-free diet. This, of course, would not solve the problem of having an inability to digest proteins, as proteins are found in vegetables, grains, eggs, and dairy as well.

The same could occur with fat or sugar, where people stay away from foods containing these components because of the way they feel after consuming them. Over time, if people continue to consume foods that their bodies are unable to digest properly, they may experience a deterioration in overall health. Let's look at some of the primary digestive enzymes and how they can affect our health.

The primary digestive enzymes include:

protease	enzymes secreted by the stomach (such as pepsin) whose catalytic function is to break down proteins
amylase	first-contact enzyme in the saliva that catalyzes starch into sugars
lipase	enzyme released by the pancreas to help break down fats

cellulase	enzyme that is not produced by humans When we eat plant matter, we rely on our gut flora to ferment it in our large intestine in order to make some of the nutrients bioavailable. The rest acts as a bulking agent in our stool. Cellulase is produced by various fungi, protozoa and bacteria that naturally have the capability to break down the cellulose, or cell wall, of plant matter. Supplementing with cellulase enables us to gain more nutritive matter from the plant foods we consume.
sucrase	a group of enzymes secreted in the small intestine that turn sucrose into the simple sugars glucose and fructose
lactase	an enzyme secreted in the small intestine that breaks down the simple milk sugar lactose
phytase	an enzyme that catalyzes the hydrolysis of phytic acid, a form of phosphorous found in grains and oil seeds, and releases it in usable form; helps with production of B vitamins.[15]

Protease Deficiency

The digestion of proteins with protease helps create acidity in the blood. Much attention has focused recently on the benefits of reducing acidity in the body, to create an alkaline state. There are diets and water ionizers, supplements and exercise plans all aimed at decreasing overall acidity in your body. Unfortunately, unless you are suffering from acidosis (a condition where there is too much acid in the body), too much alkalinity can create its own problems. When protein is not digested properly, this can create alkaline reserves that are secreted in the urine, taxing the kidneys. These alkaline reserves have been said to create a state of anxiety. As with anything, balance is key ("Protease Deficiency Conditions" 2016).

Protease, with the help of pepsin (an enzyme that is activated by hydrochloric acid in the stomach), breaks down the peptide bonds in protein foods, which then liberates the amino acids, making them absorbable through the wall of the small intestine. Proteins are made of chains" of amino acids linked together by peptide bonds. Protease breaks those "links," releasing

---

[15] Marie, 2016.

freed amino acids. The process of breaking down a cell via enzymatic or other processes is called lysis. Proteases do not digest us because the proteins in the cells of our bodies are tightly coiled. Proteases are most effective on loosely coiled proteins, such as those found in cooked foods (Erkmen 2016). We also have a natural protection via the mucosal lining in our digestive tract that prevents proteases from coming into contact with our living cells. If we did not have that lining, then we might incur some injury. If you've ever gotten sores in your mouth from eating pineapple— the affected area might turn white and then become sore—that is because pineapple contains a protease called bromelain that has started to work on breaking down cells inside your mouth. This powerful effect is one reason why bromelain is a highly popular meat tenderizer.

Proteases have been studied for their therapeutic effects. Beyond helping us digest our food, proteases have been shown to aid in reducing inflammation following injury, surgery, or strenuous exercise. Proteases break down the cellular walls of pathogenic bacteria and viruses as well. This is one of the mechanisms by which certain drugs are able to disrupt viral and bacterial activity. Parasites, bacteria, and fungi all contain proteins that, in some form, are digestible by proteases. With enzymes breaking down toxins, cellular debris, and undigested proteins in the blood, this allows the immune system to focus more effectively on immediate needs to attack targets such as bacterial, viral, or parasitic invasion.

Enzyme therapy has been shown the anti-inflammatory, anti-infectious, and antitumor capabilities of proteases when given to patients suffering from breast and colon cancers as well as plasmacytoma (Gonzales 2016).

One of the many reasons protein digestion is so important is that protein is necessary to carry protein-bound calcium in the blood. Other minerals and hormones survive in the blood to reach their target organs effectively by being bound to carrier proteins.

Calcium-binding proteins play a major role in cell functioning, such as learning, memory, and homeostasis. People who have insufficient levels of protein-bound calcium are more prone to diseases, like arthritis and osteoporosis, because when the blood lacks protein, it cannot efficiently transport calcium, causing the body to draw calcium from bones in order to maintain homeostasis, or the body's natural tendency to seek and maintain balance (Lee 2013). University of Michigan researchers used zebrafish embryos to show how low levels of calcium can contribute to the type of abnormal cell growth in the colon that can lead to cancerous tumor formation, suggesting that a deficiency in protease could potentially be a causal factor in the development of colon cancer (Bailey 2013).

People who take excessive amounts of calcium carbonate supplements tend to throw their bodies further off balance by continually increasing the pH (decreasing the acidity) of their bodies. This sort of ionic calcium is not as efficiently carried by the blood because it requires a certain amount of acidity in order to be absorbed. A lack of overall acidity has been shown to cause anxiety and other mood disorders (Kim 2014). About half of the protein you digest is converted to sugar. For some, incomplete digestion of proteins can lead to low blood sugar, and swings in blood sugar can result in swings in mood.

Albumen and globulin are the two main proteins found in blood. In the body, water follows protein. If there is inadequate protein in the blood, water tends to be drawn to tissue in order to find protein. This can contribute to edema (swelling), fluid in the ears, easy bruising, muscle wasting, fatigue, and inadequate blood clotting. Protease has also been shown to help eliminate blood clots (Cichoke 1992).

Symptoms of Low Blood Protein
brittle nails
nails with ridges on them
scaly skin
hair loss
skin rash
slow wound healing
depression
lethargy
fatigue
edema
bruising
clotting[16]

Supplementation with protease is tolerated well by most people. The only people who may be sensitive to protease supplementation are those with hiatal

---

[16]   "Total Serum Protein," 2016.

hernia, gastritis, ulcers, or any other condition where the mucosal lining of the stomach has been compromised and cannot tolerate more acidity.

Taking a protease supplement with meals will help you more completely digest protein. A protease supplement taken in between meals is absorbed through the mucosa cells in the small intestine and taken into blood circulation. It has been shown to work as a sort of "blood cleanser," breaking down viral and bacterial debris (Cichoke 1999). Since bacteria, fungi, and parasites are all made of protein, protease helps the immune system to break down these forms. And since viruses and cancer cells are protected by protein, protease can aid the immune system in fighting these as well. Some studies even indicate that high doses of protease may also decrease concentrations of heavy metal in the blood. Normally the liver produces selective protease inhibitors and distributes those to tissues like lungs, where it protects the local tissues from being digested by the protease. Genetic deficiency or defects in the structure of these protease inhibitors can render the individual vulnerable to proteases digesting tissues of vital organs in their own body, leading to illness or eventual death. One such deficiency of protease natural inhibitors is alpha 1 chymotrypsin inhibitor ("Alpha 1"), a syndrome in which those who are genetically vulnerable can develop a gradual decrease of liver production of protease inhibitors that results in gradual loss of lung or other vital organ tissues, leading to premature dysfunction or death. Persons with normal genetic structuring and production of these protease inhibitors are resistant to damaging effects of protease supplements. Individuals with a history of this disorder in their family obviously should not take protease supplements.

Protease Deficiency Symptoms		
anxiety	low blood sugar	kidney problems
back problems	candida	bacterial and viral infections
constipation	gingivitis	hearing loss
parasites	insomnia	water retention
cancer	arthritis	high blood pressure

Amylase Deficiency

Amylase is an enzyme that is present in saliva and produced by the pancreas. It is responsible for digesting dead white blood cells as well as breaking down carbohydrates or polysaccharides (complex sugars) into simple sugars or monosaccharides. There are three principal dietary monosaccharides—glucose, fructose, and galactose—that are absorbed directly into the bloodstream during digestion (Cichoke 1999).

Glucose is a simple sugar found in plants and is the body's primary energy source through a process called aerobic respiration, the release of energy from glucose in the presence of oxygen. Blood levels of glucose are measured as an indicator or preindicator of diabetes (Shipman 1993).

Fructose is a simple sugar found in plants (and honey) that is most commonly processed into table sugar. It is the sweetest of all naturally occurring carbohydrates. Fructose can either be found as a monosaccharide or as a disaccharide when bound to glucose (becoming sucrose). Fructose is directly absorbed into the small intestine, whereas sucrose requires catalyzation by the enzyme sucrase, which cleaves the two sugars into its component parts of glucose and fructose so that they can be absorbed by the intestine and enter the bloodstream through the hepatic portal vein toward the liver (Shipman 1993).

Galactose is a monosaccharide that, when joined with glucose, forms lactose. Galactose is manufactured in small quantity by the body in order for the mammary glands to be able to produce lactose (milk sugar).

Some studies have shown a positive correlation between low levels of amylase and decreased plasma insulin levels and insulin resistance in middle-aged adults (Muneyuki 2012). Amylase levels in the blood rise when the pancreas is compromised or when amylase binds to protein, causing a condition called macroamylasia, where the amylase is unable to break down white blood cells and causes these bound entities that are too big for the kidneys to process efficiently. This causes levels of amylase in the urine to decrease, while blood levels of amylase increase.

There are other factors that can lead to amylase deficiency. Among those are liver disease, cystic fibrosis, and most commonly, fat intolerance.

Fat-intolerant individuals do not have the ability to break down oils and fats in their diet. Fat intolerance can be global or specific, meaning some people may be unable to process just milk fats or oils or meat fat (Kerr 2015). People with this inability tend to stock their diet full of carbohydrates, which may overwhelm their system and result in low amylase production. People who do not have a fat intolerance but who eat a high-carbohydrate diet could experience the same effect.

Symptoms of Fat Intolerance	
acid reflux	heartburn
nausea	diarrhea
bloating	frothy, foul-smelling stool[17]
excessive flatulence	

Amylase digests dead white blood cells. When you are low in amylase, you are a candidate for blood-sugar imbalances, hypoglycemia, type-2 diabetes, carbohydrate cravings, and allergies.

Amylase has antihistamine properties which help people ward off allergic reactions to things like bug bites, bee stings, pollen, and poison ivy.

Allergic reactions occur when our immune system responds to an allergen by releasing histamine, a substance that dilates blood vessels, making the walls more permeable and therefore allowing blood fluids to enter, causing swelling of the affected area. A second type of allergic response occurs when histamine causes contraction of smooth muscle, as is the case when airways constrict to reduce breath volume during an asthma attack. Histamines are also involved in the inflammatory response in the body.

Histamines are much more than an annoyance that causes inflammation, swelling, and congestion. They actually play a role in at least twenty-three different functions within the body, including things like sleep-wake regulation by increasing wakefulness and preventing sleep. Antihistamines are traditionally known to cause drowsiness because they cross the blood-brain barrier and block histamine in the brain. Newer antihistamines are designed not to cross the barrier, therefore not having an effect in the brain on sleep-wake regulation. Histamine helps stimulate acid production in the stomach, protects against stress and convulsion, plays a role in erection and sexual dysfunction and schizophrenia, and is currently being studied as a treatment for multiple sclerosis.

Everyone has a level of tolerance for histamine. It is common for most people to have allergic response in the springtime, when there is a

---

17   Kerr, 2015.

proliferation of airborne allergens, but other factors can lower a person's threshold—stress, temperature changes, excessive sunlight an overload of environmental toxins, certain medications, or even a diet consisting of too many histamine releasing foods.

Histamine-Containing Foods		
alcoholic beverages	eggplant	spinach
smoked fish	fermented foods	tomatoes
avocados	mushrooms	vinegar
aged or fermented cheeses	processed meats	yogurt[18]
cider	soured-milk products	
dried fruits	breads high in yeast content	

Symptoms of Histamine Intolerance		
allergy symptoms	heartburn/reflux	irritated or itchy eyes
compulsive behaviors	hiccups	joint pain
dark circles under eyes	high libido	skin conditions (eczema, hives)
digestive issues	hyperactivity	tight chest, panic attacks
fatigue	hypotension	tachycardia
frequent urination	insomnia	
headaches	irritability	

There are two mechanisms at play when a person becomes intolerant to histamine. The first is an insufficient level of an enzyme called diamine oxidase. The other is a lack of function of the enzyme N-methyl transferase, an enzyme that converts norepinephrine to epinephrine. N-methyl transferase requires a methyl group to function, and some people have factors that interfere with methylation, which may cause those people to have higher levels of histamine. Quercetin is a supplement that can help by reducing histamine release and also because it is a methyl donor. SAM-e is another supplement that has helped some with this issue (Kresser 2013).

---

[18]   "Foods That Contain Histamine," 2016.

But this brings us back to amylase. The body releases amylase in response to histamines because amylase plays an anti-inflammatory role. If histamines run high in your body, you could possibly deplete your body's ability to produce amylase over time, creating a deficiency that leaves you unable to process starches and sugars efficiently.

You can now see how there might be an asthma-sugar intolerance connection.

Amylase (Digests Carbohydrates) Deficiency Symptoms		
allergies	cold hands and feet	depression
mood swings	neck and shoulder aches	fatigue
skin problems	hot flashes	PMS
hypoglycemia	allergy to bug bites	bee sting allergy
asthma	herpes outbreaks	blood sugar imbalances[19]

Lipase Deficiency

Triglycerides, or normal fats, are formed when three fatty acids are bound together with an alcohol called glycerol. Lipase is the enzyme known for breaking down dietary fats into these component parts in order to make them absorbable in the small intestine.

Fat constitutes about 40 percent of the Western diet, but our bodies also make triglycerides from carbohydrates (simple and complex sugars and starches) that we consume. In fact, a low-carbohydrate diet has been shown to decrease triglycerides in the blood (Last 2006).

Triglycerides travel in our blood and are stored in our cells, but when a triglyceride needs to move into or out of a cell, it must first be separated from the glycerol via a process called esterification, where the three fatty acids are removed from the glycerol backbone. Lipase is important in this process, as cell permeability allows nutrients to enter the cell and waste products to exit (Clark 2003).

---

[19]   "Physical Symptoms Common to Digestive Enzyme Deficiency, 2016.

Fatty acids are important for many functions throughout the body, most importantly energy storage. Whenever glucose is not available for energy production, the body will turn to fatty acids to do the job instead. This is the basis for a ketogenic diet, which relies on very low carbohydrate consumption in order to turn the body to fat-burning mode. This type of diet has been used to treat difficult epilepsy in children but is currently receiving a lot of attention as a weight-loss strategy (Klein 2010).

There is not just one type of lipase manufactured in the human body. Fat digestion begins in the stomach with lingual lipases that are secreted by the parotid and Ebner's glands at the back of the tongue. Lingual lipase, along with bile (a sort of detergent that breaks the fats into smaller molecules), helps to begin the process of digestion of fats in the stomach (such as the fats in milk). People low in hydrochloric acid tend not to make enough bile in order to complete this process. As mentioned earlier, an inadequate production of hydrochloric acid can be due to a protease deficiency and a lipase deficiency.

Pancreatic lipase is secreted by the pancreas and released in the duodenum, where it converts triglycerides into monoglycerides and fatty acids. The liver secretes bile salts, which are stored in the gallbladder and then released into the duodenum. These emulsify fats and convert larger units into much smaller units that lipase can more easily access and break down for uptake by the small intestine. There, triglycerides are transformed into lipoprotein complexes which, in turn, are transported to the lymph and then into the blood for transport for storage or structural purposes. When there is an excessive accumulation of storage triglycerides, people may develop fatty liver, insulin resistance, and type-2 diabetes (Kawano 2013).

Various Lipases Found in the Human Body		
Name	Location	Description
bile salt-dependent lipase	pancreas, breast milk	Helps with digestion of fat.
pancreatic lipase	digestive juice via pancreas	In conjunction with a protein, colipase, this is the most prevalent lipase in human digestion.

lysosomal lipase	intracellular: lysosome	Exists in acidic environment of about pH 5. Digests unwanted materials in the cytoplasm from inside and outside of the cell.
hepatic lipase	endothelium	Post digestion, acts on remaining lipids in the blood to regenerate LDL.
lipoprotein lipase	endothelium	Acts on triacylglycerides in the blood so cells can take up freed fatty acids.
hormone-sensitive lipase	intracellular	The long form is expressed in steroidogenic tissues such as testis, for steroid hormone production. The short form is expressed in body fat, where it hydrolyzes stored triglycerides to free fatty acids.
gastric lipase	digestive juice	In infants functions at a near-neutral pH to help digestion of lipids.
endothelial lipase	endothelium	Key player in HDL metabolism.
lingual lipase	salivary glands	Functions at pH 3.5–6. Secreted by the parotid and Ebner's glands at the back of the tongue.[20]

People can become lipase deficient in a number of ways. Some people experience gallbladder malfunction and are truly fat intolerant. Fat is one of the most difficult nutrients to break down, and the inability to digest fat can wreak havoc with insulin metabolism, causing issues with glucose transport. These people tend to eat more sugar in place of the fat they are avoiding in their diet. Other people are complex-carbohydrate intolerant and do the opposite—they avoid sugar in place of high amounts of fat.

---

[20] Wikipedia, 2016.

Conditions Arising from Lipase Deficiency	
diabetes	high triglycerides
difficulty losing weight	varicose veins
glucosuria	vitamin deficiency (A, D, and E)
high cholesterol	xanthelasma
high blood pressure	

Most Americans live in fear of fat (Cohl 1997). We are taught to believe that fat is the enemy, when actually, the right kinds of fats are essential to optimal health (Chen 2014). We are designed to crave fats. Many nutrients, such as beta carotene, lutein, vitamins A, D, E, and K, are all fat soluble, which means that the vitamins are absorbed through the intestine with the assistance of dietary fats, and excess vitamins are stored in body fat. Water-soluble vitamins, by contrast, dissolve in water, and whatever is not used by the body is excreted in the urine. For this reason, water-soluble vitamins require more consistent intake, whereas fat-soluble vitamins carry with them the risk of hypervitaminosis, or the overavailability of a particular fat-soluble vitamin or vitamins. The amount stored can, over time, become toxic to the body.

The trick is not to avoid fat but to eat the right kinds of fats (Chen 2014). The American diet is laden with hydrogenated oils and unhealthy saturated fats. The consumption of good fats is necessary for proper function of the nervous system, hormone production, and inflammation control.

The USDA guidelines for 2015[21], in fact, do not recommend a low-fat diet. The new guidelines recommend that 35 percent of the calories you consume should come from healthy fats. The old guidelines generally told us how to avoid fat (consuming fat-free or 1-percent milk, consuming low-fat cheeses) without teaching which fats we should seek out. The new guidelines are more comprehensive, but then again, the story of what to eat and what to avoid seems to be constantly changing, with marketing, political, and dietary emphasis on one food type and ignoring others. There is "good cholesterol" or "all cholesterol is to be avoided"; yet cholesterol is important to normal cell function. Dairy is "harmful," or dairy is "one of nature's most perfect

---

[21]   US Department of Health and Human Services and US Department of Agriculture. 2015–2020 Dietary Guidelines for Americans, 8th Edition. December 2015. Available at http://health.gov/dietaryguidelines/2015/guidelines.

foods." Sugar substitutes "prevent obesity," or sugar substitutes "result in greater weight gain over time." For example, in this final statement, the first phrase is the result of simplistic and nonscientific thinking that has crept into recent legislation, and the second phrase is the actual result of repeated scientific studies. By taking sugar substitutes over long periods, the body adjusts to the lack of sugars by compensating and changing its metabolism, resulting in actual weight gain in spite of not ingesting sugars.

Simply put, there are two main types of fats: saturated and unsaturated. Generally speaking, unsaturated fats have been shown to lower cholesterol levels and reduce the risk of heart disease. Unsaturated fats can be broken down further into two subgroups: monounsaturated and polyunsaturated.

Monounsaturated fats are part of what gets the Mediterranean Diet so much attention. These types of fats are typically liquid at room temperature, solidify when refrigerated, and can be found in abundance in the traditional diets consumed in Mediterranean countries—lots of nuts, olives, olive oil, and fish—and are thought to decrease the risk of heart disease, based on the low instance of heart disease in countries that consume more of these types of fats over certain others, such as saturated fats.

Foods Rich in Monounsaturated Fat		
olives	almonds	sesame seeds
avocados	brazil nuts	pumpkin seeds
hazelnuts	cashews	olive, canola, and peanut oils
macadamia nuts	pecans	pistachios[22]
peanuts	nut butters	

Polyunsaturated fats have been shown to help lower cholesterol and triglyceride levels and can be found in seeds, nuts, leafy greens, fish, algae, and krill. These fats are liquid at room temperature and, unlike with monounsaturated fats, remain liquid even when chilled ("Polyunsaturated Fats" 2015).

The fats that guidelines suggest be limited, if not avoided, are saturated fats and trans fats.

Saturated fats are found in animal products such as meat, dairy, and eggs, and also in coconut and palm oils. The USDA 2005 dietary guidelines

---

[22]   "Monounsaturated Fats," 2015.

recommend that saturated fat should be less than 10 percent of the total calories you consume per day. Some evidence suggests that saturated fats increase the risk of certain cancers.

Trans fats were developed by manufacturers in order to create a higher melting point for certain oils, turning liquid oils into solid oils via a process called hydrogenation. During hydrogenation, extra hydrogen atoms are added to liquid oils in order to increase the melting point. Why? Because the melting point of coconut oil, for instance, is seventy-six degrees Fahrenheit. Products manufactured with coconut oil would then begin to melt once they reach that temperature, which they may very well do in the transportation process from manufacturing plant to retail outlet. Hydrogenation, aside from extending shelf life, also stabilizes flavor. This process was developed during a time when saturated fat (such as is found in butter) was being heralded as evil and people were avoiding it, not knowing the hidden dangers lurking in the new substitute. Manufacturers eventually realized that trans fats lasted longer before going rancid, and this suited their goals, despite ill health effects on the consumers.

The irony of trans fat is that while manufacturers and consumers alike were avoiding butter, these new trans fats that they were consuming were acting like butter inside their bodies—clogging arteries by raising LDL or "bad" cholesterol, which contributes to the buildup of plaque in arteries and may contribute to type-2 diabetes. It is estimated that at one time, as many as 95 percent of packaged cookies and 100 percent of commercial crackers contained trans fats ("Shining the Spotlight on Trans Fats" 2016). Now, thanks to a rule that took effect on January 1, 2006, trans fats must be on the label right along with saturated and unsaturated fats. This transparency has caused many food manufacturers to change their formulations in order to eliminate trans fats and caused heightened consumer awareness as people learned to recognize trans-fat ingredients such as hydrogenated or partially hydrogenated oils.

Where Trans Fats Lurk		
vegetable shortening	cereals	chips
margarine	candies	salad dressing[23]
crackers	cookies (baked goods)	
fried food	granola bars	

---

[23]   Kirkpatrick, 2015.

The good fat/bad fat debate has been going on for decades—probably for at least as long as there have been processed foods, and the pendulum is swinging again. A recent study published in the *Annals of Internal Medicine* concluded that evidence did not support a higher incidence of heart disease in those who consumed more saturated fat compared to those who consumed less (Chowdhury 2014). In many ways, this makes total sense. Without a veritable smorgasbord of processed foods at our fingertips, we are meant to be low-carb and fat-burning machines.

Prior to the development of agriculture, routine widespread carbohydrate consumption was unheard of (Cordain 2005). Carbohydrate consumption among humans was opportunistic (such as stumbling upon a maple tree leaking sap) at best until grain cultivation and storage allowed people to remain in one location. People who relied on hunting and fishing existed mainly on protein but more importantly on saturated fat for sustenance. Humans cannot sustain themselves for long periods of time solely on lean protein. In fact, there is a phenomenon called "rabbit starvation," where people trying to subsist on notoriously lean rabbit meat would in essence starve even though gorging themselves (Bilsborough 2006). Arctic peoples would, at times, discard an animal that was too lean or would give lean meat to their dogs, saving the fat and fattiest portions of meat for themselves. In fact, scientists have studied the health and dietary habits of people in the Arctic who subsisted on such a diet and found their rates of heart disease and cancer to be a fraction of those found in Western society. Some scientists claim this is because wild-caught fish and game have a higher instance of Omega-3 fatty acids, and this may very well play a part in what has come to be known as "the Inuit Paradox" (Gadsby 2004). Regardless, it is interesting to note that these people far from shied away from fat. Put in perspective, this is one of the oldest ways of eating throughout human history, and it only makes sense that our bodies are designed for it.

Contrary to popular belief, fat is actually the preferred fuel for the heart. In fact, fat malabsorption is positively correlated with heart failure, and a 2011 study done by Case Western Reserve School of Medicine found that patients put on a high-fat diet showed significant cardiac mechanical function over patients on the typically suggested low-fat diet (Sharma 2007).

Does this mean it's okay to go out and gorge on burgers and fries? No. It just means that eating the proper fats and having the ability to process those fats is beneficial to overall health.

Lipase not only digests fat but also balances fatty acids and helps with absorption of fat-soluble vitamins. People deficient in lipase tend to find losing weight difficult and tend to have higher cholesterol and triglycerides which, over time, can contribute to heart disease. In fact, decreased cell permeability due to lipase deficiency disallows the free movement of nutrients (such as glucose) into the cell and waste products out. This is a contributing factor to diabetes, and the risk of heart disease in people with diabetes tends to be two to four times higher than for people without diabetes (Yuan 2007).

Lipase (Digests Fat) Deficiency Symptoms		
high cholesterol	cardiovascular problems	arthritis
cystitis	diarrhea	bladder problems
chronic fatigue	obesity	acne
diabetes	aching feet	gallstones
hay fever	prostate problems	psoriasis
urinary weakness	constipation	Meniere's disease[24]
muscle spasms		

Cellulase Deficiency

Cellulase is one digestive enzyme that breaks down the fiber in our diet. Because our bodies do not produce cellulase, we need help breaking down cellulose, a polysaccharide, into monosaccharides or simple sugars such as glucose that can be converted into energy by the body. Cellulase is either obtained from consuming raw foods such as whole grains, fruits, and vegetables, or from supplements; otherwise much of the plant fiber passes through the body undigested (Senese 1997).

If a person lacks a sufficient amount of cellulase in his or her diet, this can manifest itself in the form of something called malabsorption syndrome, where the lining of the small intestine has an impaired ability to take in nutrients. This syndrome can cause gas and bloating in the short term. In the long term, as a result of this faulty digestion, some people develop neurological conditions such as facial neuralgia, Bell's palsy and tic, as well as certain food intolerances such as sugar and gluten. A lack

---

[24]   Canadian Liver Foundation, 2016.

of cellulase can also lead to candida overgrowth. The cell wall of candida contains chitin, which, being similar to cellulose in nature, is broken down by cellulase ("Enzymes: Digestive and Anti-Inflammatory" 2016).

Cellulase (Digests Fiber) Deficiency Symptoms	
candidiasis (yeast infections)	gas/bloating
acute food allergies	facial pain or paralysis[25]

Sucrase (Disaccharidases) Deficiency

Sucrase deficiency is congenital in nature and stems from several possible genetic mutations. People with sucrose-isomaltase enzyme deficiency are unable to break down table sugar and grain sugars in the small intestine. There is a high incidence of this deficiency in certain segments of the Inuit population in Alaska (Marcadier 2015).

Sucrose (fruit or table sugar) and maltose (grain sugar) are both known as disaccharides because they are comprised of two simple sugars which, during the normal process of digestion, are cleaved into their component parts. Sucrose is broken down into the simple sugars fructose and glucose, and maltose is broken down into two glucose molecules.

People are typically diagnosed with sucrose deficiency after they are weaned in infancy, when they begin consuming foods and beverages that contain complex sugars.

Sucrase (Disaccharidases) Deficiency Symptoms	
gas/bloating	cramping
diarrhea	failure to gain weight[26]
malnutrition	

The good news for children who suffer from this deficiency is that, as they get older, many children are better able to tolerate complex sugars.

---

[25]   "Enzymes: Digestive and Anti-Inflammatory," 2016.
[26]   Marcadier, 2016.

Lactase Deficiency

Similar to sucrose deficiency, lactase deficiency is another form, and the most common form, of disaccharidase deficiency. People who are lactose intolerant are unable to break lactose down into its two simple sugars, glucose and galactose. The inability to properly digest these sugars leads to gas, bloating, and diarrhea within thirty minutes to two hours after consumption of foods containing lactose. It should be noted that the FDA allows lactose as a food additive (typically as a sweetener) without labeling, so, for severely lactose-intolerant people, this can be very frustrating ("NMPF Wants Dairy Ingredients Problem Fixed" 2014).

People are typically born[27] with the ability to digest lactose so that they can breastfeed, but over time, enzyme levels decline. The rate of decline differs in various populations. For instance, people of Asian and Native American descent have a higher instance (75 to 90 percent) of lactose intolerance than those from Northern European backgrounds (25 percent). It is estimated that 75 percent of the world's population is lactose intolerant (Newcomer 1978).

There are two types of lactose intolerance:

Primary: the development after childhood of low levels of lactase; and

Secondary: the development of situational lactose intolerance after acute illness, which may cause damage to the mucosal lining of the small intestine.

Lactase Deficiency Symptoms	
gas/bloating	cramping
diarrhea	nausea/vomiting
asthma	rumbling/gurgling[28]

---

[27] Congenital lactose intolerance does exist, but it is extremely uncommon (Upton 2007).

[28] "Lactose Intolerance," 2016.

There are several factors that can contribute to a decrease in the production of digestive enzymes: inflammation in the digestive tract caused by food allergies, age, heavy alcohol consumption, low stomach acid, and—a big one—chronic stress (Gerstmar 2012). For me, atrophic gastritis caused low stomach acid and therefore decreased enzyme production.

While some people might note a deficiency in just one digestive enzyme (for instance, lactose intolerance), others might suffer from severe digestive distress stemming from multiple deficiencies. These deficiencies can mask themselves as chronic conditions such as frequent colds and sinus infections, IBS (irritable bowel syndrome), allergies, and fatigue. Just look at the list of symptoms for each enzyme deficiency earlier in this chapter, and you can imagine the havoc a combination deficiency can wreak on an individual's health!

We need enzymes to break our food into amino acids from proteins, simple sugars from carbohydrates, and cholesterol from fats, in order to absorb nutrients. A breakdown in any one of these processes leaves our nutritional profile incomplete.

The good news is that if you suspect you might have an enzyme deficiency, there are many types of digestive-enzyme supplements on the market that you can try in order to aid your digestion. I chose MRM Digest All for its wide spectrum of coverage, as well as its inclusion of herbal digestive aids. This one worked for me, but everyone is different.

There are two types of digestive enzyme supplements: plant enzymes and animal enzymes. I don't recommend animal-based enzymes, because they tend to be unstable, and the health of the source animal cannot be confirmed with absolute certainty. Plant-based enzymes are generally safer and more stable.

How you supplement will depend on your own needs. Aside from aiding digestion, digestive enzymes, taken on an empty stomach, help to bolster your immune system by entering the bloodstream and breaking down the protein coating on certain viruses, which enables your immune system to more quickly destroy them.

Some people have multiple types of enzyme supplements they take depending on the foods they have eaten. What you choose will depend on your individual needs and may require a certain amount of trial and error.

As always, the best source of enzymes is your diet. Incorporating enzyme-rich, whole, organic, unprocessed foods into your diet is an excellent first step to reclaiming your health, as those foods have all the enzymes you need to digest them already inside of them. An avocado, for instance, has more lipase (for fat digestion) than an apple, which is high in amylase (for sugar digestion).

Ideally these enzyme-rich foods should be consumed raw or lightly steamed in order to keep those healthy enzymes intact. Exceptions would be beans, seeds, grains, and nuts, which contain enzyme inhibitors. These inhibitors can be deactivated by cooking, soaking, or sprouting.

Within two weeks of starting enzyme treatment, my symptoms went away. I lost an additional ten pounds after starting a lower-carbohydrate diet and was, for the most part, symptom free. I still have a weak LES from previous damage and have the occasional minor reflux, but it is uncommon. Now, after engineering my way to healing, I maintain a low-fat and low-carbohydrate diet; I avoid chocolate, alcohol, and citrus. I rarely take probiotics or digestive enzymes, unless I have eaten an unusually heavy meal. Aside from mild belching when I am under stress, I remain happy and, for the most part, symptom free.

I hope that my journey can be a gift for you in your own healing process.

I have developed some nutrition tips I would like to share with the reader.

Chapter 8

Dysfunction of the Lower Esophageal Sphincter

After my indigestion symptoms were resolved, I began to concentrate on my reflux. I understand it is not a functional error; it is rather a structural dysfunction. I understand my intermittent reflux is from the loose, damaged valves caused by *H. pylori*. The lower esophageal sphincter (LES) is a smooth muscle structure, like an automatic thick rubber band to block the food from the stomach to the esophagus. From endoscopic pathology, I know I have severely damaged valves. The rubber band is loose, and the valves cannot tighten when needed.

I reviewed my Final Pathology Report of Endoscopy again:

> The endoscope report is finalized. It reveals no hiatal hernia, mild inactive chronic gastritis, atrophic appearance mucosa with erythema in the antrum compatible with atrophic gastritis, impaired lower esophagus valve (sphincter), HILL grad 3 gastroesopgeal valve. (Grade I and II valves were classified as normal valves; grades III and IV valves as considered abnormal valves)

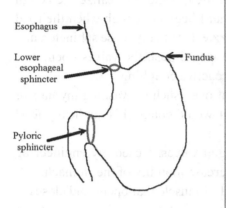

Grade I: Prominent fold of tissue along the lesser curvature that was closely apposed to the endoscope.

Grade II: Fold was present, but there would be periods of opening and rapid closing around the endoscope.

Grade III: Fold was not prominent, and the endoscope was not gripped tightly by the tissues.

Grade IV: There was no fold, and the lumen of the esophagus gaped open, allowing the squamous epithelium to be viewed from below.

It had damaged my lower esophageal valve. Damage is rated on a scale of one to four; mine was grade three. It would explain the GI reflux and the hiatal hernia.

I first had reflux in 1999, as I mentioned in the chapter on GERD. I had some symptoms that I did not know about that were from reflux, as I gradually realized. One of my reflux symptoms is reflux laryngitis. I had beautiful voice, was in singing group, and always had performances. I noticed after a 1999 treatment for H. pylori. My voice was frequently hoarse. I was unable to raise my voice, even to call my patients from the waiting room. At the holiday party, I could not sing.

I had a frequent cough. I first noticed when I was lying down before sleep, I would cough. I thought it may be from the dust of my bed, so I began to clean my bed. I changed my down pillow that I thought I was responsible. I cleaned the dust from the bed's headboard. I still coughed in bed. I then cleaned the lamp on the nightstand. It was very dusty. After I cleaned, it seemed the cough was relieved to some degree. I did not know it was from positional reflux. If you have a normal sphincter from the lower esophagus, the valve will prevent it from happening.

I also noticed that sometimes when I was in the car, I would cough. I blamed my husband for not keeping the car clean; it was full of dust.

Because the symptoms were so intermittent, I did not realize the cough was from reflux. One day I realized that I began to cough when the road was bumpy. I had the answer to the puzzle. Due to my loose sphincter, any small increase in abdominal pressure would push the valves open. The reflux from the stomach would cause reactive coughing.

I noticed it sometimes when I bent over, such as washing my hair or picking up something from the floor, I would cough. If I ate heavy food and went to bed early, it was also the case.

I know it is difficult to fix damaged valves. I used my engineering method to bolster my digestion and increase mobility of the stomach.

As stated above, the LES is a band of muscle that opens and closes at the base of the esophagus and is responsible for maintaining a pressure barrier between the esophagus and the contents of the stomach. If the LES weakens, it cannot completely close after food passes into the stomach, which allows for stomach contents to regurgitate into the esophagus. Several things can weaken the LES, including dietary, hormonal, neural, and lifestyle factors.

Normal subjects typically only experience reflux during normal transient lower esophageal sphincter relaxations or during LES relaxation after swallowing. People with GERD tend to experience more reflux during TLESRs alone, indicating that some patients with GERD have more transient LES relaxations (TLESRs) compared to people who do not have GERD (De Giorgi 2006).

LES dysfunction can be either neurogenic or myogenic.

Neurogenic is a deficit from an autonomic nervous system dysfunction with increased tone of the acytochilinergic tone or impairment of the autonomic nerve from a condition such as diabetes.

Myogenic can be secondary from neurogenic or damage to the sphincter from chronic inflammation or from *H. pylori*, as in my case.

Factors Decreasing LES Pressure	
foods	chocolate
	alcohol
	peppermint
	caffeine
	high-fat meals

hormones	cholecystokinin
	progesterone
	secretin
	glucagon
	polypeptide
	vasoactive intestinal
	polypeptide
neural agents	adrenergic agonists
	adrenergic antagonists
	anticholinergic agents
other	theophylline
	smoking
	morphine
	meperidine
	calcium-blocking agents
	diazepam
	dopamine[29]

LES hypotension is a condition where the LES is in a constant state of relaxation. This can be found in patients with scleroderma and can result in esophagitis, Barrett's esophagus, and peptic strictures.

My LES dysfunction is a structural impairment of the sphincter. It has suffered long-term damage from *H. pylori* and long-term reflux.

Treatment for Damaged LES

I tried some simple tips to control heartburn, but the only one that was suitable for me was number one.

1. Avoid foods and beverages that affect LES pressure or irritate the esophageal lining, including fried and fatty foods, peppermint, chocolate, alcohol, coffee, citrus fruit and juices, and tomato products.
2. Lose weight if overweight.
3. Stop smoking.
4. Elevate the head of the bed six inches.
5. Avoid lying down for two to three hours after eating.

---

[29] Kahrilas, 2016.

6.   Take an antacid.

I became very frustrated. There was no sufficient sphincter muscle tone in my LES. Besides paying attention to not eating heavy meals, I avoided bending. What else could I do? Finally, I decided that the best method of addressing my symptoms was to prevent further damage by reducing inflammation and by increasing local blood circulation to promote tissue repair, even if just a little. I began to massage my LES area every day. I used an infrared device on my LES area. My reflexes began to show improvement. I decided I would also throw acupuncture into the mix.

Dr. Gao's Recipes for Digestive and Overall Health

Five Super Soup Weight Loss

It includes eight to ten dry shiitake mushrooms; five to six black wood ears, dry or fresh; two fresh carrots and half bulk of fresh celery. With the above, add five to seven cups of water to stew one hour to make clear soup. Drink one cup once or twice a day.

Five benefits of the soup: 1. Lowers blood pressure. 2. Lowers cholesterol. 3. Beneficial for blood-sugar metabolism. 4. Increases immune system against cancer. 5. Helps lose weight. (I lost ten pounds over three months. Several of my patients had similar effects.)

Daily Antioxidant Cookies

Lots of food has natural nutritional and health benefits. When you put them together, it is called functional food.

Dark-color food has more antioxidant values, ORAC (oxygen radical absorbance capacity, a method of measuring antioxidant capacities in biological samples in vitro). High-ORAC food is relatively high in antioxidants. I use high-concentrate fruit extract (cranberry, blueberry, roseberry, papaya, goji) with nuts, or mocha tea powder or sesame powder with almond oil or avocado oil to make nutritional cookies that can be taken two at each meal to maintain a healthy body.

Bibliography

Aaron Cohl. 1997. *Are We Scaring Ourselves to Death?* Macmillan. https:// books.google.com/books/about/Are_We_Scaring_Ourselves_to_ Death.html?id=2X2eoXrRN3MC.

"Acid Reflux (GERD) Statistics and Facts." 2016. *Healthline.* Accessed May 12. http://www.healthline.com/health/gerd/statistics.

"Acidic Environments." 2016. *Acidic.* Accessed May 24. http://serc.carleton. edu/microbelife/extreme/acidic/index.html.

Alcock, Joe, Carlo C. Maley, and C. Athena Aktipis. 2014. "Is Eating Behavior Manipulated by the Gastrointestinal Microbiota? Evolutionary Pressures and Potential Mechanisms." *BioEssays* 36 (10): 940–49, doi:10.1002/bies.201400071.

Ali, A. A., and I. M. Roushdy. 1998. "Fermentation of Milk Permeate by Proteolytic Bacteria for Protease Production." *Applied Biochemistry and Biotechnology* 74 (2): 85–93.

Last, Allen R., M.D., M.P.H., and Stephen A. Wilson, M.D., M.P.H. 2006. "Low-Carbohydrate Diets - American Family Physician." *American Family Physician.* June 1. http://www.aafp.org/afp/2006/0601/p1942. html.

Cichoke, Anthony J. 1992. *The Complete Book of Enzyme Therapy.* Penguin. https://books.google.com/books/about/The_Complete_ Book_of_Enzyme_Therapy.html?id=eqkYpqkYPngC.

Arnold, Rudolf. 2007. "Diagnosis and Differential Diagnosis of Hypergastrinemia." *Wiener Klinische Wochenschrift* 119 (19–20): 564–69. doi:10.1007/s00508-007-0878-0.

"Artichokes Help an Ailing Liver | LiverSupport.com." 2016. Accessed May 23. http://www.liversupport.com/artichokes-help-an-ailing-liver/.

"Articles - Allergy & Immunology Associates of Michigan - W, Bloomfield MI, Livonia MI." 2016. Accessed May 27. http://www.michiganallergy. com/food_and_histamine.shtml.

"Association of Dietary, Circulating, and Supplement Fatty Acids With Coronary Risk: A Systematic Review and Meta-Analysis." 2016. Accessed May 27. http://wphna.org/wp-content/ uploads/2014/08/2014-03_Annals_of_Int_Med_Chowdhury_et_al_ Fat_and_CHD_+_responses.pdf.

Austin, Gregory L., Michelle T. Thiny, Eric C. Westman, William S. Yancy, and Nicholas J. Shaheen. 2006. "A Very Low-Carbohydrate Diet Improves Gastroesophageal Reflux and Its Symptoms." *Digestive Diseases and Sciences* 51 (8): 1307–12. doi:10.1007/s10620-005-9027-7.

Kim, Ben, M.D. 2014. "The Truth About Alkalizing Your Blood." *Dr. Ben Kim*. July 4. http://drbenkim.com/ph-body-blood-foods-acid-alkaline. htm.

Beuth, Josef. 2008. "Proteolytic Enzyme Therapy in Evidence-Based Complementary Oncology: Fact or Fiction?" *Integrative Cancer Therapies* 7 (4): 311–16. doi:10.1177/1534735408327251.

"Bifidobacteria : MedlinePlus Supplements." 2016. *U.S. National Library of Medicine*. Accessed May 25. https://www.nlm.nih.gov/medlineplus/ druginfo/natural/891.html.

"Bile | Biochemistry | Britannica.com." 2016. Accessed May 23. http:// www.britannica.com/science/bile.

Bland, Michael V., Salim Ismail, Jack A. Heinemann, and Jacqueline I. Keenan. 2004. "The Action of Bismuth against Helicobacter Pylori Mimics but Is Not Caused by Intracellular Iron Deprivation." *Antimicrobial Agents and Chemotherapy* 48 (6): 1983–88. doi:10.1128/ AAC.48.6.1983-1988.2004.

Nazario, Brunilda. 2015. "Vitamin B12 Deficiency: Causes, Symptoms, and Treatment." *WebMD*. Accessed July 23. http://www.webmd.com/ food-recipes/guide/vitamin-b12-deficiency-symptoms-causes.

Bures, Jan, Jiri Cyrany, Darina Kohoutova, Miroslav Förstl, Stanislav Rejchrt, Jaroslav Kvetina, Viktor Vorisek, and Marcela Kopacova. 2010. "Small Intestinal Bacterial Overgrowth Syndrome." *World Journal of Gastroenterology : WJG* 16 (24): 2978–90. doi:10.3748/ wjg.v16.i24.2978.

Center for History and New Media. n.d. "Zotero Quick Start Guide." http:// zotero.org/support/quick_start_guide.

James, Charles W. 2016. "NutritionGang.com | Common Symptoms of Digestive Enzyme Deficiency." Accessed May 25. http://nutritiongang. com/digestive-enzyme-deficiency/.

Kresser, Chris. 2013. "Headaches, Hives, and Heartburn: Could Histamine Be the Cause?" *Chris Kresser*. January 25. http://chriskresser.com/ headaches-hives-and-heartburn-could-histamine-be-the-cause/.

"Congenital Sucrase-Isomaltase Deficiency (CSID)." 2016. *International Foundation for Functional Gastrointestinal Disorders*. Accessed May

27. http://iffgd.org/other-disorders/congenital-sucrase-isomaltase-deficiency-csid.html.

Cordain, Loren, S. Boyd Eaton, Anthony Sebastian, Neil Mann, Staffan Lindeberg, Bruce A. Watkins, James H. O'Keefe, and Janette Brand-Miller. 2005. "Origins and Evolution of the Western Diet: Health Implications for the 21st Century." *The American Journal of Clinical Nutrition* 81 (2): 341–54.

"Could Histamine Be Sabotaging Your Digestive Health? | Diets for Autism, ADHD, Allergies, Autoimmune and Digestive Disorders." 2016. Accessed May 27. http://peelingbacktheonionlayers.com/could-histamine-be-sabotaging-your-digestive-health/.

Cross, Amanda J, Michael F Leitzmann, Mitchell H Gail, Albert R Hollenbeck, Arthur Schatzkin, and Rashmi Sinha. 2007. "A Prospective Study of Red and Processed Meat Intake in Relation to Cancer Risk." *PLoS Medicine* 4 (12). doi:10.1371/journal.pmed.0040325.

Dabos, K. J., E. Sfika, L. J. Vlatta, and G. Giannikopoulos. 2010. "The Effect of Mastic Gum on Helicobacter Pylori: A Randomized Pilot Study." *Phytomedicine: International Journal of Phytotherapy and Phytopharmacology* 17 (3–4): 296–99. doi:10.1016/j.phymed.2009.09.010.

Darbro, Benjamin W., Brian K. Petroelje, and Gary V. Doern. 2009. "Lactobacillus Delbrueckii as the Cause of Urinary Tract Infection." *Journal of Clinical Microbiology* 47 (1): 275–77. doi:10.1128/JCM.01630-08.

De Giorgi, F, M Palmiero, I Esposito, F Mosca, and R Cuomo. 2006. "Pathophysiology of Gastro-Oesophageal Reflux Disease." *Acta Otorhinolaryngologica Italica* 26 (5): 241–46.

Delgado, Amanda. 2015. "Hiatal Hernia." *Healthline.* September 26. http://www.healthline.com/health/hiatal-hernia.

den Besten, Gijs, Karen van Eunen, Albert K. Groen, Koen Venema, Dirk-Jan Reijngoud, and Barbara M. Bakker. 2013. "The Role of Short-Chain Fatty Acids in the Interplay between Diet, Gut Microbiota, and Host Energy Metabolism." *Journal of Lipid Research* 54 (9): 2325–40. doi:10.1194/jlr.R036012.

Houston, Devin, Ph.D. 2016. "What Your Doctor May Not Know About Enzymes » Houston Enzymes." *Houston Enzymes.* Accessed May 25. http://www.houston-enzymes.com/learn/articles/doctor-may-not-know.php.

"Diabetes, Heart Disease, and Stroke." 2016. *National Institute of Diabetes and Digestive and Kidney Diseases.* Accessed May 27. http://www. niddk.nih.gov/health-information/health-topics/Diabetes/diabetes-heart-disease-stroke/Pages/index.aspx.

"Digestive System, Information about Digestive System." 2016. *Advameg.* Accessed May 24. http://www.faqs.org/health/topics/65/Digestive-system.html.

Editor, Website. 2016. "Physical Symptoms Common to Digestive Enzyme Deficiency." *Healthynewage.com.* January 28. http://www. healthynewage.com/symptoms/.

"Enterohepatic Circulation | Definition of Enterohepatic Circulation by Medical Dictionary." 2016. *The Free Dictionary/Medical Dictionary.* Accessed May 25. http://medical-dictionary.thefreedictionary.com/ enterohepatic+circulation.

"Enzyme | Biochemistry." 2016. *Encyclopedia Britannica.* Accessed May 25. http://www.britannica.com/science/enzyme.

"Enzymes: Digestive & Anti-Inflammatory." 2016. *DC Nutrition.* Accessed May 27. https://www.dcnutrition.com/miscellaneous/Detail. CFM?RecordNumber=144.

"Evaluation and Management of Dyspepsia - American Family Physician." 2016. Accessed May 23. http://www.aafp.org/afp/1999/1015/p1773. html.

"Fecal Transplantation (Bacteriotherapy) | Johns Hopkins Division of Gastroenterology and Hepatology." 2016. *Johns Hopkins Medicine.* Accessed May 25. http://www.hopkinsmedicine.org/ gastroenterology_hepatology/clinical_services/advanced_endoscopy/ fecal_transplantation.html.

Festi, Davide, Ramona Schiumerini, Leonardo Henry Eusebi, Giovanni Marasco, Martina Taddia, and Antonio Colecchia. 2014. "Gut Microbiota and Metabolic Syndrome." *World Journal of Gastroenterology : WJG* 20 (43): 16079. doi:10.3748/wjg.v20.i43.16079.

Gadsby, Patricia, and Leon Steele. 2004. "The Inuit Paradox | DiscoverMagazine.com." *Discover Magazine.* October 1. http:// discovermagazine.com/2004/oct/inuit-paradox.

Senese, Fred. 2016. "General Chemistry Online: FAQ: Chemistry of Everyday Life: What Is Cellulose?" *General Chemestry Online.* Accessed May 27. http://antoine.frostburg.edu/chem/senese/101/ consumer/faq/what-is-cellulose.shtml.

Gastroenterology, Greenwich Village. 2016. "Helicobacter Pylori & Gastritis Symptoms and Treatment Information." Accessed May 24. http://www.starpoli.com/helio.

"Gastroesophageal Reflux Disease - Very Detailed Technical Article | eMedMD.com." 2016. Accessed May 23. http://www.emedmd.com/content/gastroesophageal-reflux-disease-very-detailed-technical-article.

"Gastroparesis." 2016. Accessed May 27. http://www.niddk.nih.gov/health-information/health-topics/digestive-diseases/gastroparesis/Pages/facts.aspx.

"GBMC Test Dictionary." 2016. Accessed May 12. http://www.specialtylabs.com/clients/gbmc/books/display.asp?id=141.

"GERD Symptoms - Mayo Clinic." 2016. Accessed May 23. http://www.mayoclinic.org/diseases-conditions/gerd/basics/symptoms/con-20025201.

Brigitte, Gilbert, Mustapha Rouis, Sabine Griglio, Lionel de Lumley, and Paul-Michel Laplaud. 2001. "Lipoprotein Lipase (LPL) Deficiency: A New Patient Homozygote for the Preponderant Mutation Gly188Glu in the Human LPL Gene and Review of Reported Mutations: 75 % Are Clustered in Exons 5 and 6." *Annales de Génétique* 44 (1): 25–32. doi:10.1016/S0003-3995(01)01037-1.

Gorbach, Sherwood L. 1996. "Microbiology of the Gastrointestinal Tract." In *Medical Microbiology*, edited by Samuel Baron, 4th ed. Galveston (TX): University of Texas Medical Branch at Galveston. http://www.ncbi.nlm.nih.gov/books/NBK7670/.

Gupta, R., N. Gupta, and P. Rathi. 2004. "Bacterial Lipases: An Overview of Production, Purification and Biochemical Properties." *Applied Microbiology and Biotechnology* 64 (6): 763–81. doi:10.1007/s00253-004-1568-8.

Hadley, Caroline. 2006. "The Infection Connection: Helicobacter Pylori Is More than Just the Cause of Gastric Ulcers—it Offers an Unprecedented Opportunity to Study Changes in Human Microecology and the Nature of Chronic Disease." *EMBO Reports* 7 (5): 470. doi:10.1038/sj.embor.7400699.

"H. Pylori Infection - Mayo Clinic." 2016. Accessed May 23. http://www.mayoclinic.org/diseases-conditions/h-pylori/basics/definition/CON-20030903?p=1.

"H. Pylori Infection Causes - Mayo Clinic." 2016. Accessed May 23. http://www.mayoclinic.org/diseases-conditions/h-pylori/basics/causes/con-20030903.

Haristoy, Xavier, Karine Angioi-Duprez, Adrien Duprez, and Alain Lozniewski. 2003. "Efficacy of Sulforaphane in Eradicating Helicobacter Pylori in Human Gastric Xenografts Implanted in Nude Mice." *Antimicrobial Agents and Chemotherapy* 47 (12): 3982–84. doi:10.1128/AAC.47.12.3982-3984.2003.

"Hiatal Hernia Causes, Symptoms, And ..." 2012. *Memorialhermann.* November 11. http://www.memorialhermann.org/digestive/hiatal-hernia/.

Hill, M. J. 1997. "Intestinal Flora and Endogenous Vitamin Synthesis." *European Journal of Cancer Prevention: The Official Journal of the European Cancer Prevention Organisation (ECP)* 6 Suppl 1 (March): S43-45.

Horne, Steven. 2010. "Hiatal Hernia: An Overlooked Cause of Disease." *East West Healing.* June 23. http://eastwesthealing.com/hiatal-hernia-an-overlooked-cause-of-disease/.

Houston, Devin, Ph.D. 2016. "What Your Doctor May Not Know About Enzymes » Houston Enzymes." Accessed May 27. http://www.houston-enzymes.com/learn/articles/doctor-may-not-know.php.

"H.Pylori/Low Stomach Acid: Nutritional Treatment/Causes, Remedies, Prevention." 2016. Accessed May 27. http://www.acu-cell.com/dis-hpy.html.

Huwez, Farhad U., Debbie Thirlwell, Alan Cockayne, and Dlawer A.A. Ala'Aldeen. 1998. "Mastic Gum Kills Helicobacter Pylori." *New England Journal of Medicine* 339 (26): 1946–1946. doi:10.1056/NEJM199812243392618.

"Indigestion and Your Digestive System." 2016. *WebMD.* Accessed May 25. http://www.webmd.com/heartburn-gerd/indigestion.

"Is A Cellulase Enzyme Deficiency Making You Sick?" 2016. *Digestive Health Guide.* Accessed May 27. http://digestivehealthguide.com/cellulase-enzyme/.

Jensen, Henrik R, Martin F Laursen, Dorte L Lildballe, Jens B Andersen, Ebba Nexø, and Tine R Licht. 2011. "Effect of the Vitamin B12-Binding Protein Haptocorrin Present in Human Milk on a Panel of Commensal and Pathogenic Bacteria." *BMC Research Notes* 4 (June): 208. doi:10.1186/1756-0500-4-208.

Clark, Jim. 2003. "Esterification - Alcohols and Carboxylic Acids." *Chemguide.* http://www.chemguide.co.uk/organicprops/alcohols/esterification.html.

Marie, Joanne. 2016. "What Are the Functions of Amylase, Protease and Lipase Digestive Enzymes." *SF Gate.* Accessed May 25. http://healthyeating.sfgate.com/functions-amylase-protease-lipase-digestive-enzymes-3325.html.

Johnson, Shannon. 2015. "Stomach Ulcer: Causes, Symptoms & Diagnosis." *Healthline.* August 25. http://www.healthline.com/health/stomach-ulcer.

Mercola, Joseph, M.D. 2011. "Enzymes: Food That Slow Nearly Every Inflammatory Disease." *Mercola.com.* August 21. http://articles.mercola.com/sites/articles/archive/2011/08/21/enzymes-special-report.aspx.

Kalliomäki, Marko, and Erika Isolauri. 2003. "Role of Intestinal Flora in the Development of Allergy." *Current Opinion in Allergy and Clinical Immunology* 3 (1): 15–20. doi:10.1097/01.all.0000053262.39029.a1.

Kandil, Tharwat S., Amany A. Mousa, Ahmed A. El-Gendy, and Amr M. Abbas. 2010. "The Potential Therapeutic Effect of Melatonin in Gastro-Esophageal Reflux Disease." *BMC Gastroenterology* 10: 7. doi:10.1186/1471-230X-10-7.

Kawano, Yuki, and David E. Cohen. 2013. "Mechanisms of Hepatic Triglyceride Accumulation in Non-Alcoholic Fatty Liver Disease." *Journal of Gastroenterology* 48 (4): 434–41. doi:10.1007/s00535-013-0758-5.

Kirkpatrick, Kristin, MS, RD, and LD. 2015. "Avoid These 10 Foods Full of Trans Fats." *Health Essentials from Cleveland Clinic.* July 10. https://health.clevelandclinic.org/2015/07/avoid-these-10-foods-full-of-trans-fats/.

Klein, Pavel, Jaromir Janousek, Arkady Barber, and Randi Weissberger. 2010. "Ketogenic Diet Treatment in Adults with Refractory Epilepsy." *Epilepsy & Behavior: E&B* 19 (4): 575–79. doi:10.1016/j.yebeh.2010.09.016.

Kusters, Johannes G., Arnoud H. M. van Vliet, and Ernst J. Kuipers. 2006. "Pathogenesis of Helicobacter Pylori Infection." *Clinical Microbiology Reviews* 19 (3): 449–90. doi:10.1128/CMR.00054-05.

"Lactobacillus: MedlinePlus Supplements." 2016. *U.S. National Library of Medicine*. Accessed May 25. https://www.nlm.nih.gov/medlineplus/druginfo/natural/790.html.

"Lactose Intolerance - Mayo Clinic." 2016. *Mayo Clinic*. Accessed May 19. http://www.mayoclinic.org/diseases-conditions/lactose-intolerance/basics/definition/con-20027906.

"Lactose Intolerance: Background, Pathophysiology, Etiology." 2016, April. http://emedicine.medscape.com/article/187249-overview#a4.

"Lansoprazole Side Effects in Detail - Drugs.com." 2016. Accessed May 23. http://www.drugs.com/sfx/lansoprazole-side-effects.html.

Bailey, Laura. 2013. "Zebrafish Help Decode Link between Calcium Deficiency and Colon Cancer." *University of Michigan News*. December 13. http://www.ns.umich.edu/new/releases/21861-zebrafish-help-decode-link-between-calcium-deficiency-and-colon-cancer.

Lesbros-Pantoflickova, Drahoslava, Irène Corthésy-Theulaz, and André L. Blum. 2007. "Helicobacter Pylori and Probiotics." *The Journal of Nutrition* 137 (3): 812S–818S.

"Lipase." 2016. *Wikipedia, the Free Encyclopedia*. https://en.wikipedia.org/w/index.php?title=Lipase&oldid=721990258.

"Lipases - Lipase - Enzyme That Breaks Down Fats - Diet and Health.net." 2016. Accessed May 27. http://www.diet-and-health.net/Supplements/Lipase.html.

Lita Lee, Ph.D. 2009. "Arthritis." *Litalee.com*. March 13. http://www.litalee.com/shopexd.asp?id=132.

"Low Protein in Blood | New Health Guide." 2016. Accessed May 25. http://www.newhealthguide.org/Low-Protein-In-Blood.html.

Lowe, M. E. 2002. "The Triglyceride Lipases of the Pancreas." *The Journal of Lipid Research* 43 (12): 2007–16. doi:10.1194/jlr.R200012-JLR200.

Lowe, Robert C. 2006. "Medical Management of Gastroesophageal Reflux Disease." *GI Motility Online*, May. doi:10.1038/gimo54.

"Lysosomal Acid Lipase Deficiency (LALD)." 2016. Accessed May 27. http://www.liver.ca/liver-disease/types/Lysosomal_Acid_Lipase_Deficiency_(LALD).aspx.

Marcadier, Julien L., Margaret Boland, C. Ronald Scott, Kheirie Issa, Zaining Wu, Adam D. McIntyre, Robert A. Hegele, Michael T. Geraghty, and Matthew A. Lines. 2015. "Congenital Sucrase–isomaltase Deficiency: Identification of a Common Inuit Founder

Mutation." *CMAJ : Canadian Medical Association Journal* 187 (2): 102. doi:10.1503/cmaj.140657.

Chen, Michael A., M.D. 2014. "Dietary Fats Explained: MedlinePlus Medical Encyclopedia." *Medline Plus*. August 12. https://www.nlm. nih.gov/medlineplus/ency/patientinstructions/000104.htm.

Kerr, Michael, and Jacquelyn Cafasso. 2015. "Malabsorption Syndrome." *Healthline*. September 26. http://www.healthline.com/health/ malabsorption.

Mignon, M. 1998. "What Are the Myogenic and Neurogenic Components of the Lower Esophageal Sphincter High Pressure Zone at Rest?" *OESO Knowledge*. May. https://www.hon.ch/OESO/books/Vol_5_ Eso_Junction/Articles/art009.html.

Miller, T, L., and M. J. Wolin. 1979. "Fermentations by Saccharolytic Intestinal Bacteria." *The American Journal of Clinical Nutrition* 32 (1). 164–72.

Mittal, Ravinder K., and Raj K. Goyal. 2006. "Sphincter Mechanisms at the Lower End of the Esophagus." *GI Motility Online*. doi:10.1038/ gimo14.

Reinagel, Monica. 2014. "Are Soil-Based Organisms Beneficial?" *Quick and Dirty Tips*. April 1. http://www.quickanddirtytips.com/health-fitness/ trends-fads/are-soil-based-organisms-beneficial.

"Monounsaturated Fats." 2016. Accessed May 27. http://www.heart. org/HEARTORG/HealthyLiving/HealthyEating/Nutrition/ Monounsaturated-Fats_UCM_301460_Article.jsp#.V0h9LNdx1ro.

Muneyuki, Toshitaka, Kei Nakajima, Atsushi Aoki, Masashi Yoshida, Hiroshi Fuchigami, Hiromi Munakata, San-e Ishikawa, et al. 2012. "Latent Associations of Low Serum Amylase with Decreased Plasma Insulin Levels and Insulin Resistance in Asymptomatic Middle-Aged Adults." *Cardiovascular Diabetology* 11: 80. doi:10.1186/1475-2840-11-80.

Bilsborough, S. and Mann, N. 2016. "A Review of Issues of Dietary Protein Intake in Humans. - PubMed - NCBI." Accessed May 27. http://www. ncbi.nlm.nih.gov/pubmed/16779921.

Nakajima, Kei, Tohru Nemoto, Toshitaka Muneyuki, Masafumi Kakei, Hiroshi Fuchigami, and Hiromi Munakata. 2011. "Low Serum Amylase in Association with Metabolic Syndrome and Diabetes: A Community-Based Study." *Cardiovascular Diabetology* 10 (April): 34. doi:10.1186/1475-2840-10-34.

Namias, Nicholas. 2003. "Honey in the Management of Infections." *Surgical Infections* 4 (2): 219–26. doi:10.1089/109629603766957022.

Gonzales, Nicholas, M.D. 2016. "Enzyme Therapy and Alternative Cancer Treatment - Dr. Nicholas Gonzalez." *Dr-Gonzales.com*. Accessed May 25. http://www.dr-gonzalez.com/history_of_treatment.htm.

"NMPF Wants Dairy Ingredients Problem Fixed in FDA 'Added Sugar' Definition | National Milk Producers Federation." 2016. Accessed May 19. http://www.nmpf.org/latest-news/press-releases/aug-2014/nmpf-wants-dairy-ingredients-problem-fixed-fda-%E2%80%98added-sugar%E2%80%99.

Nzeako, Basil C, and Faiza Al-Namaani. 2006. "The Antibacterial Activity of Honey on Helicobacter Pylori." *Sultan Qaboos University Medical Journal* 6 (2): 71–76.

Orrhage, K., E. Sillerström, J. -Å. Gustafsson, C. E. Nord, and J. Rafter. 1994. "Binding of Mutagenic Heterocyclic Amines by Intestinal and Lactic Acid Bacteria." *Mutation Research/Fundamental and Molecular Mechanisms of Mutagenesis* 311 (2): 239–48. doi:10.1016/0027-5107(94)90182-1.

Osman Erkmen, and T.F. Bozoglu. 2016. *Food Microbiology*. Vol. 1. Wiley Publishers. https://books.google.com/books/about/Food_Microbiology.html?id=pxDRCwAAQBAJ.

"Pathogenesis of Helicobacter Pylori Infection." 2016. Accessed May 23. https://www.researchgate.net/profile/Johannes_Kusters/publication/6938890_Pathogenesis_of_Helicobacter_pylori_Infection_Clin_Microbiol_Rev/links/00b4951914af1c367e000000.pdf.

"Physiology Of The Small Intestine, Part 1." 2016. Accessed May 25. https://jonbarron.org/article/physiology-small-intestine-part-1#.V0XQw9dx1ro.

Kahrilas, P.J. 2016. "What Is Basically Wrong with the LES in Reflux Disease?" *OESO Knowledge*. Accessed May 27. http://www.hon.ch/OESO/books/Vol_3_Eso_Mucosa/Articles/ART005.HTML.

Pollan, Michael. 2013. "Say Hello to the 100 Trillion Bacteria That Make Up Your Microbiome." *The New York Times*, May 15. http://www.nytimes.com/2013/05/19/magazine/say-hello-to-the-100-trillion-bacteria-that-make-up-your-microbiome.html.

"Polyunsaturated Fats." 2016. Accessed May 27. http://www.heart.org/HEARTORG/HealthyLiving/HealthyEating/Nutrition/Polyunsaturated-Fats_UCM_301461_Article.jsp#.V0h9gNdx1ro.

"Preventative Concept: Acid Alkaline Imbalances." 2016. Accessed May 23. http://preventativeconcept.com/library/other/acid_alkaline.shtml.

"PROTEASE DEFICIENCY: ENZYMES.COM." 2016. *Enzymes.com.* Accessed May 25. http://www.enzymes.com/protease_deficiency.html.

Rees, Alan. 1997. *Consumer Health USA.* Vol. 2. Oryx Press.

Reference, Genetics Home. 2016. "Congenital Sucrase-Isomaltase Deficiency." *Genetics Home Reference.* Accessed May 24. https://ghr. nlm.nih.gov/condition/congenital-sucrase-isomaltase-deficiency.

"Related Diseases - H. Pylori Stomach Infection Symptoms and Treatment." 2016. Accessed May 23. http://www.medicinenet.com/helicobacter_pylori/related-conditions/index.htm.

Richter, J. E. 2004. "Effect of Helicobacter Pylori Eradication on the Treatment of Gastro-Oesophageal Reflux Disease." *Gut* 53 (2): 310. doi:10.1136/gut.2003.019844.

Rochlitz, Steven, Ph.d. 2013. *Hiatal Hernia Syndrome/Vagus Nerve Imbalance.* Human Ecology Balancing Science. https://books.google. com/books/about/Hiatal_Hernia_Syndrome_Vagus_Nerve_Imbal. html?id=SZt0oAEACAAJ.

Roussos, Anastasios, Nikiforos Philippou, and Konstantinos I. Gourgoulianis. 2003. "Helicobacter Pylori Infection and Respiratory Diseases: A Review." *World Journal of Gastroenterology* 9 (1): 5–8.

"Saccharomyces Boulardii : MedlinePlus Supplements." 2016. *U.S. National Library of Medicine.* Accessed May 25. https://www.nlm. nih.gov/medlineplus/druginfo/natural/332.html.

Sarah Pope. 2012. "At What Temperature Are Food Enzymes Destroyed?" *The Healthy Home Economist.* July 18. http://www.thehealthyhomeeconomist. com/at-what-temperature-are-food-enzymes-destroyed/.

"Scientific-Report-of-the-2015-Dietary-Guidelines-Advisory-Committee. pdf." 2016. Accessed May 27. http://health.gov/dietaryguidelines/2015-scientific-report/pdfs/scientific-report-of-the-2015-dietary-guidelines-advisory-committee.pdf.

Sharma, Naveen, Isidore C. Okere, Monika K. Duda, David J. Chess, Karen M. O'Shea, and William C. Stanley. 2007. "Potential Impact of Carbohydrate and Fat Intake on Pathological Left Ventricular Hypertrophy." *Cardiovascular Research* 73 (2): 257–68. doi:10.1016/j. cardiores.2006.11.007.

"Shining the Spotlight on Trans Fats – The Nutrition Source – Harvard T.H. Chan School of Public Health." 2016. Accessed May 27. http://www. hsph.harvard.edu/nutritionsource/transfats/.

"Siberian Pine Nut Oil: How a Folk Remedy Found Its Way into Scientific American." 2010. *Examiner.com.* February 17. http://www.examiner. com/article/siberian-pine-nut-oil-how-a-folk-remedy-found-its-way-into-scientific-american.

Sircus, Mark Sircus Dr Mark, Ac., OMD, DmDirector International Medical Veritas Association Doctor of Oriental, and Pastoral Medicine. 2014. "Function of the Vagus Nerve." *Dr. Sircus.* December 26. http:// drsircus.com/medicine/function-vagus-nerve.

Steele, Eurídice Martínez, Larissa Galastri Baraldi, Maria Laura da Costa Louzada, Jean-Claude Moubarac, Dariush Mozaffarian, and Carlos Augusto Monteiro. 2016. "Ultra-Processed Foods and Added Sugars in the US Diet: Evidence from a Nationally Representative Cross-Sectional Study." *BMJ Open* 6 (3): e009892. doi:10.1136/bmjopen-2015-009892.

Horne, Steven. 2009. *How to Identify and Correct a Hiatal Hernia: Part 1.* https://www.youtube.com/watch?v=hrdNfaanpIs.

"The Potential Therapeutic Effect of Melatonin in Gastro-Esophageal Reflux." 2016. Accessed May 23. http://www.medscape.com/ viewarticle/717460_5.

"Three Enzyme Catagoroes." 2016. Bio Set. *Perfect Health Body and Mind.* Accessed May 25. http://www.perfecthealthnow.com. au/bioset/what-is-bioset/enzymes-information-and-function/ enzyme-information/.

"Vitamin B12: MedlinePlus Medical Encyclopedia." 2016. Accessed May 25. https:https://www.nlm.nih.gov/medlineplus/ency/article/002403. htm.

Vlahos, James. 2011. "Is Sitting a Lethal Activity?" *The New York Times,* April 14. http://www.nytimes.com/2011/04/17/magazine/mag-17sitting-t.html.

"Ways to Increase Stomach Acid Production." 2016. *Branch Basics.* Accessed May 24. https://branchbasics.com/ ways-to-increase-stomach-acid-production/.

Westerterp, Klaas R. 2004. "Diet Induced Thermogenesis." *Nutrition & Metabolism* 1: 5. doi:10.1186/1743-7075-1-5.

"What Everybody Ought To Know (But Doesn't) About Heartburn & GERD." 2010. *Chris Kresser.* March 29. https://chriskresser.com/what-everybody-ought-to-know-but-doesnt-about-heartburn-gerd/.

Chey, William, and Brennan Spiegel. 2010. "Proton Pump Inhibitors, IBS, and Small Intestinal Bacterial Overgrowth." *Medscape.* http://www.medscape.com/viewarticle/723772.

Wright, Steven. 2012. "Hypochlorhydria: 3 Common Signs of Low Stomach Acid." *SCD Lifestyle.* June 12. http://scdlifestyle.com/2012/06/hypochlorhydria-3-common-signs-of-low-stomach-acid/.

Yancy, W. S., D. Provenzale, and E. C. Westman. 2001. "Improvement of Gastroesophageal Reflux Disease after Initiation of a Low-Carbohydrate Diet: Five Brief Case Reports." *Alternative Therapies in Health and Medicine* 7 (6): 120, 116–19.

Yuan, George, Khalid Z. Al-Shali, and Robert A. Hegele. 2007. "Hypertriglyceridemia: Its Etiology, Effects and Treatment." *CMAJ : Canadian Medical Association Journal* 176 (8): 1113–20. doi:10.1503/cmaj.060963.

Zayouna, Nafea. 2014. "Atrophic Gastritis: Background, Pathophysiology, Epidemiology," December. http://emedicine.medscape.com/article/176036-overview.

Printed in the United States
by Bookmasters

Printed in the United States
By Bookmasters